Geri Schneider Winters

Best-selling author "Applying Use Cases: A Practical Guide"

Why Agile
is *Failing*
at Large
Companies

(and what you can do so it won't fail at yours)

Ty yn Goch
Forrest
Publications
Albion, California

Published by Ty yn Goch Forrest Publications in 2015
First edition; First printing

Design and writing ©2015 Geri Schneider Winters
Cover design by Leigh St. John and Geri Schneider Winters
Author cover photo by Landers Photography, San Antonio, Texas

Any suggestions in this book are based on the author's own experience. They may or may not be relevant to your particular situation. The author and publisher do not guarantee any results you may achieve by following the suggestions in this book. Examples and stories are typically composites of several similar events and do not describe a specific person or company.

ISBN: 978-0-9967426-4-1

For additional book resources or to contact the author go to
www.AgileIsFailing.com

As Always

For Jason

Contents

The Big Five Engineering Practices 63

Acknowledgements

Super big thanks to Leigh St. John, friend and coach extraordinaire! All alone it is hard to stick with a big project such as writing a book. Leigh kept me accountable for my deadlines in a most supportive, non-judgmental way. This book could have remained on my hard drive (like the 18 other books I just have not quite finished writing). You have this book in your hands because of Leigh.

And thank you to Greg, the persona to whom this book is written. Greg is a composite of people I have known, but really came to life during this project. He is so real to me and Leigh, she called me one night to say she had met him!

Greg represents all of you who want to know what Agile will mean at your company. Greg kept me focused on the needs of the executive, reminding me that he does not care how the teams work, he cares about what a change to Agile will mean to the different parts of the company. He wants to understand what all these consulting companies are talking about, and he wants to know about the hidden issues, the surprising things that make Agile really hard to do.

While I have done the writing, the ideas in this book have been hashed out over many years with many people. In particular, I have been privileged to be part of a very special tribe. As individuals and together, we observe carefully, think deeply, discuss honestly, research diligently, test and learn scientifically, and write openly in a very synergistic way. So these special thanks are to Thomas Meloche, Greg Fournier, Michael Russell, Kyle Griffin, Andrew Breese, and Sarah Perry for all the discussions and sharing over the years.

A Letter to Greg

Dear Greg –

First I must thank you for bringing me into your company to listen to your business executives express their concerns, misconceptions, and questions about what Agile means to them.

You had all read about Scrum, eXtreme Programming, Kanban, SAFe, Lean Startup, and so on, but all the things you read did not answer the business questions you had about the impact Agile would have on the business.

You correctly identified that this impact was far more than describing a Product Owner role, that Agile would have a profound impact throughout your company if it were to provide the business agility, the ability to quickly respond to market changes, that Agile promises.

You asked me "Is it worth it?" and "Will I lose my job?"

This is something you need to determine. It may not be worth it (or at least not for the whole company). Being an agent of change, you do risk your job unless you have strong support from the executives above you.

Agile is a broad term encompassing many practices. What you are most concerned with is not really software development practices but rather business agility and how to get there. In general how agile your company becomes, and in what areas, should be a business decision based on some cost/benefit analysis.

In large companies, every part does not have to be able to pivot quickly to respond to changes in your market. Some things just do not change that fast, so changing those areas to be able to respond quickly when they do not need to may not be worth the investment. On the other hand, for those fast changing parts of your company, business agility may be the difference between the life and death of some or all of your business.

To be able to move fast, you will need to make changes in product development, but also in perhaps surprising places – procurement, accounting systems, reporting structures, and human resources are just a few examples.

Are those areas able to change to support your view of business agility? Do they need to change to support your view of business agility? I will give you information in this book that will help you find the answers to these questions for your company.

Business agility is enabled by the way people work. For example, you do not get business agility when all decisions have to be approved by several layers of management. To get business agility a company has to adopt agile practices in pivotal parts of the business. Are you willing and able to change the way people work in order to be a more agile business?

What I have put together in this book is a description of a number of agile practices that can be done throughout your company. Some can be done by anyone, some are specific to software development. Some can be started with very limited impact and expanded when they have proven their worth. Others will require large changes in your company to implement. For each practice I outline the potential benefits and impact to your company so you can decide if the potential benefits are high enough to justify the cost of making the change.

I will not tell you that you are not agile unless you do some specific thing. Agile is a continuum, not all or nothing; you can be more or less agile based on the needs of your business and market. Be proud of anything you can do to support greater business agility for your company and do not be concerned that you are not doing every practice.

Approach your agile journey as a cafeteria where you have a number of options and you choose those that bring the most value for a cost you are willing to pay - a cost in time, money, and political capital.

Geri

Introduction

Why should you listen to me? I'm an industry insider. I have helped companies in the Fortune 200 who want to adopt Agile (or its predecessor practices) for more than 20 years. Press reports and case studies to the contrary, I am aware of exactly one successful company wide Agile transformation in the Fortune 200. That was a European company and the transformation was not recent.

I know what has been written up as successes. Some I have been involved with, in some cases I have talked to the people who were there. I see the best face that is put on these stories for public consumption. I know the reality behind the stories.

While I have not seen widespread Agile adoption inside large companies, I have seen pockets of success within these companies. If executive management has patience, they could grow those pockets into large scale success. Without executive management interest and active support over many years, these pockets of success gradually fade away and it is back to business as usual. A large scale transformation in a large company can easily take 5-7 years. Will you have support for that long?

Instead of trying to "implement Agile company wide", a more feasible (and faster) approach is to select a small number of practices that can be implemented without requiring buy-in from a lot of different departments and interest groups. Show success with those practices and use that success to get buy-in from more people.

I have seen this approach work over and over. It takes vision and patience, but is much more successful than flashy approaches such as training 600 people to work in a new way overnight (without first putting in place the supporting structures that will let them work in a new way).

You do not tend to see case studies talking about how implementing a small change saved the company 5-10% in costs. But add up enough of those small changes and 5-10% improvements, and you have something very significant over time.

In the past couple of decades, most large companies tried to gain efficiency by focusing on optimizing the individual. What the Toyota Way, Lean, Lean Startup, and the Menlo Way have all proven is that focusing instead on optimizing throughput gives both the greatest efficiency and the ability to quickly change focus when needed.

When you make the end-to-end flow as short as possible, you get market feedback very quickly which provides you the information you need to change. If your end-to-end flows inside your company are also as short as possible (planning, procurement, staff allocation, hiring, onboarding, etc.) then you can also quickly make changes in those areas. As you review the practices in this book keep in mind that while you get benefit from optimizing the work of an individual, the greatest gains come from optimizing the end-to-end flow.

Why Agile?

Implementing Agile is not actually a measurable goal. It is poorly defined and open-ended. If you want to actually achieve something, you have to determine what that something is. What do you expect to get out of implementing Agile? Some answers I have heard frequently are:

- Get more insight into what my teams are doing
- Find out earlier if we are headed down a wrong path
- Get higher quality of products
- Reduced time to market
- Better respond to user's needs
- Reduced cost of product development
- Reduced total lifetime cost of the product

- Respond quickly to changing market conditions

As a personal goal, you probably hope this will boost your career, but that goal will not sell well to others. What is important to your company? What issues do you hope to improve? What matches the company culture and values?

Do some thinking about this and also consider the fundamental risk that Agile is designed to mitigate: Are we delivering the right product, at the right time, for the right ROI? Is that question something that is important to your company leadership? If not, implementing Agile is probably not a good idea, though the practices in sections 1 and 2 make any process better so you can still bring improvements in the items in the bulleted list above without implementing the practices typically meant when people say Agile.

Determine now if Agile can even fit your company's culture, including attitudes, structures, relationships (formal and informal), metrics, and rewards (formal and informal).

Waterfall and Agile Solve Different Problems

To avoid spectacular failure, the first thing you absolutely must know, really deep down, is that a Waterfall approach to product development and an Agile approach to product development *solve different problems*. This is why it is not easy to replace one with the other. If your problems are those solved by Waterfall, then implementing Agile will cause you nothing but more problems. If your problems are those solved by Agile, then changing to Agile will ultimately be successful.

Waterfall, along with Earned Value Management (EVM) which measures its success, is designed to solve the problem of "are we delivering projects on time and on budget".

Agile, along with frequent demonstrations of working product which measures its success, is designed to solve the problem of "are we delivering the right product".

These are completely different problems, completely different questions we are answering. Now in Waterfall we still want to deliver the right product and in Agile we still want to deliver on time and on budget. But the fundamental focus is completely different.

This is a point you must be absolutely clear on if you expect to succeed with implementing Agile at your company. Are your peers in agreement that the fundamental problem is you are not delivering the right products? Or do they think the fundamental problem is that your projects are late and/or over budget? If you have both problems, which is the greater problem or of more value to solve?

Of course there are other issues to address, but this is the heart of the difference. If what you, your peers, and the company really want is to deliver the right product (especially at the right time for the right ROI), then Agile is for you. If everyone is focused on delivering projects on time and on budget (note I said project not product), then trying to implement Agile will be a very long and possibly not successful process of changing people's attitudes about what is best for the company.

You may hear the argument that delivering projects on time and on budget is how we deliver the right product. This is not at all true. I have worked for many companies who delivered every project on time and budget, and whose products were poorly received or even complete failures. I have also worked for many companies whose projects were not always on time or budget, but who delivered products that the users loved and that made a really nice return on investment (ROI) for the company. Now obviously the projects were close enough to on time and budget or the ROI would have been bad, but the projects still "failed" by EVM measures.

Agile Fails Without Executive Support

The success of adopting Agile practices is directly related to the attitude of the executive management team. Do they want the benefits enough to persevere through the transition until the changes have become part of the work practices of the company? Is this the fad du jour which will be abandoned after the next executive seminar, or will they really support change over the long term?

In a large corporation, you cannot expect even small lasting results in less than a year no matter how good your people are. This is entirely due to corporate inertia. Things just do not move that fast in a big company. You will see benefit before then, but to embed the change in the company takes time. Widespread transformation in a large corporation can take 5-7 years or more. Will the executive team be the same? Is there support from the board of directors? Will they stay the course?

Answers to these questions will help you decide up front how far you will be able to take an Agile transformation.

You could potentially get a 10-25% improvement with a couple of simple practices (such as the Big Three Management Practices) implemented throughout the company. Is that good enough? Because even though the changes are relatively simple, implementing them will be painful.

People do not want to change how they have been working. You will be asking for more accountability, and not just from implementers but from managers as well. You will be asking managers to do more than fill out a status report weekly. Many people work for large companies because they can hide. Just implementing the Big Three Management Practices will shine a light where people prefer the darkness. They will not be happy with you. And this is the easy stuff!

Decide your level of perseverance – how long do you want to do this? If you just implement a couple of relatively simple changes and get them in place widespread, lasting, and demonstrating benefit (about a year for a really big company), is that good enough? Or are you looking at a 5-7 year transformation? Will you (and the company) stick with it that long? Really? If you get a desired job change part way through, will you abandon the effort or stick with it to the end?

Successfully Transitioning to Agile

The heart of a business that wants to be responsive to its market can be described by these fundamental imperatives:

- Determine Real End User Needs
- Work on the Most Important Thing to the User First
- Deliver Incrementally
- Demonstrate Progress Transparently
- Get Feedback from Real End Users Often
- Continuously Improve

There are many different ways that these imperatives can be implemented, which is where the art and science of implementing agile practices becomes interesting.

Assuming your company is not in crisis and has time to become more agile, a slow and steady approach over time is the most effective if you want the changes to last.

- Start with a few people (influencers who will embrace change), get them to implement a couple of new practices, and let the use of the practices spread.
- Start the change with a small set of practices that will show benefit but that do not require changes in most of your corporation, and stick with implementing those practices until they are truly embedded in the company.
- Once everyone is solid on the new practices, pick practices that require more extensive change in the corporation, but not huge change, and implement as before.
- Once everyone is solid on those new benefits, work on things that require bigger changes in your corporation (if you still want to).

At each stage, add some practices, take enough time that they are embedded in the company, evaluate the benefit, and determine if you really want to do more. Keep measuring benefit, keep communicating benefit. Be sure everyone knows there are good things happening because of the new practices.

Even better from your career point of view, if you start implementing these practices with small numbers of people at the beginning, and increase the people using these practices over time, you will only look good. Starting small and ramping up is actually faster over a six month period, much faster over longer periods, and much less risky for your career.

The book is organized with the less widespread (and typically easier) changes first, and the more widespread (and typically harder) changes last. I have seen 10-25% productivity improvement with making just the easier changes, so they are definitely worth doing.

Do not be concerned about comparing the practices you adopt to the practices adopted by other companies or trying to determine who is more Agile. As you go through the journey toward greater business agility, celebrate your successes and be proud of the benefits you achieve for yourself and your company.

Remember: The goal of Agile is the right product for the users at the right time for the right ROI. Anything you do to improve in those areas means you are doing it right.

How to Read this Book

This book describes a variety of practices that can be adopted to make your company better able to adapt quickly to change in your market. Some of these practices are modern flavors of things that engineers of all kinds have done throughout history. Others are more specific to knowledge work, especially software development. Many of these practices were common in the past but have been largely forgotten due to a lack of understanding of their importance.

This is not really a book to read end-to-end. Feel free to skip around and read the parts that interest you the most. If someone is recommending specific practices, you may want to look at those practices first to see if they make sense for your company.

Sections 1 and 2 contain the practices that are likely to be the easiest to implement. You might also be interested in reading section 5 which discusses what a company that has a lot of business agility might look like. Sections 3 and 4 are a catalog of practices that may be problematical in a large company.

Section 1 of this book is the Big Three Management Practices. While these practices can be applied to any kind of work, you must do them to be able to implement any additional Agile practices. If you cannot do the Big Three Management Practices, then you will not be able to implement Agile (though you can still implement the engineering practices in Section 2).

Section 2 of this book is the Big Five Engineering Practices. The Big Five practices can be used within any software development process and most product development processes. In an environment of large teams that are geographically distributed, you need these practices to be able to become more agile as a business. If you cannot do the Big Five Engineering Practices, you will struggle over time with maintaining the Agile practices in later parts of the book, especially if your teams are distributed.

Section 3 of this book discusses eXtreme Programming, commonly called XP. These practices are specific to software development. While the XP community says all of these practices need to be done together, in real life inside a large company many of them will not be possible because of the large impact of the change on other parts of the company. Because of this, some companies find that some of the XP practices will be so expensive to implement that they are not worth the investment.

You are no longer impacting just product development, you are adopting practices that require big changes throughout your company.

22

You may decide the cost of these changes in time, money, and political capital is too high compared to the benefit received. If so, do not worry. Focus on the benefits you get from the practices in Section 1 and 2. These benefits can be quite substantial, long lasting, and beneficial to the company and your career.

Section 4 discusses additional common Agile practices that are surprisingly difficult to implement in large companies except in small pockets. Because of the relatively high cost of implementing them throughout your whole company, these are practices, along with the XP practices, that you may want to use only in parts of your company that require lightning fast change, such as with your innovation teams.

Section 5 outlines an ideal structure for a company that is truly agile and responsive to their market. Read that section, compare to your company, and think about how far you want to go. How important is business agility to your company? Which parts of your company need it and which ones do not? Will your board of directors support this kind of change? Are the benefits worth the costs, both tangible and intangible?

A Story of What Can Go Wrong

You are an executive at a large corporation. You want to bring Agile to your company because you believe it will help your company and (not coincidentally) it will help your career. If it works, it is a real win-win. If it fails, it is a real lose-lose. I want to help you and your company win.

Once upon a time there was a Vice President of a very large company who wanted to be the Chief Information Officer (CIO). Peter needed to do something impressive in the IT department to show that he was the best leader, and so he decided to implement Agile.

Peter did not make enough of an effort to find out what that really meant, so while he did many things right, other things he did very wrong. The effort failed in a spectacular way; Peter was fired and Darlene, who was not part of the Agile effort, became the CIO. Agile was a dirty word, never to be spoken within those walls again.

This really happened, and it could happen to you.

Use the information in this book to help you avoid the pitfalls and make an educated decision about whether or how much Agile to do at your company.

Section One
The Big Three
Management Practices

The minute you get away from fundamentals – whether it's proper technique, work ethic or mental preparation – the bottom can fall out of your game, your schoolwork, your job, whatever you're doing.

- Michael Jordan

An Introduction to the Practices

While we will talk about a number of "Agile" practices in this book, the Big Three Management Practices are the most important. These three things can actually make ANY work process more efficient, but are particularly important for a company that wants to be agile. These three practices are where any Agile journey should begin. They are:

1. A continuously maintained prioritized work package queue
2. Regular demonstrations of functional solutions
3. Incremental delivery of solution

These three practices get to the heart of being adaptable to market changes and delivering the right product at the right time for the right return on investment. They sound simple and they are simple.

These practices can be harder to implement in a widespread manner for companies that plan all work a year in advance and measure success by delivering exactly to plan. These Big Three Management Practices introduce flexibility which is hard to do for companies that make change difficult.

These practices are also harder to implement in a widespread way in companies structured as matrix organizations. This is because people are typically matrixed onto a project for some time, then moved to a different project. The Big Three Management practices set up a rhythm of many short delivery cycles (instead of the typical pattern of fewer longer delivery cycles) so people reassignment may be needed more frequently.

These practices are independent of the kind of solution to be developed or the work to be done. For example, these practices are commonly found in personal productivity programs. There are exceptions: frequently the manufacture of hardware is so expensive that the cost of frequent small releases far outweighs the benefit received. But for any kind of "soft" product produced by knowledge workers for the benefit of human beings, these practices are the foundation of an agile approach to developing the solution. And even for physical products, those that are relatively inexpensive to produce compared to sales price will benefit from these three practices.

The best thing about the Big Three Management Practices is that anyone can use them from individuals to teams to departments to large multi-year projects. Ideally, other parts of your organization will make some changes as well (specifically greater involvement for customers and users and new metrics for executives) because that will lead to even greater benefit, but it is not required to show improvement in delivering the right solution to the users at the right time.

I have used these practices to turn around a large multi-year failing Waterfall project that appeared to have everything going against its success. The project still remained a Waterfall project with all the Waterfall reporting and metrics. We completed successfully by every Waterfall measure and also delivered a solution that delighted the customer and the end users. That is the power of these practices.

These Big Three Management Practices when performed by one individual implementer will improve the quality of that one person's work and will improve your visibility into the progress of that work. The more people who adopt these practices, the greater the benefit. And these Big Three Management Practices make it possible to adopt the more traditional Agile practices that you read about.

Ideally, the business users will be involved with these practices, including the portfolio team. The use of these practices throughout the business hierarchy, and the accompanying change in metrics, is a bigger change but will give your company a huge boost in its ability to be an agile business.

The Big Three Management Practices are foundational to all other Agile practices. If you cannot get these three practices implemented in your company, you will not be able to implement Agile. There are some other improvements you can make in software development by implementing better engineering practices in your Waterfall projects, but you will not be able to do Agile.

Chapter 1

Continuously Maintained Prioritized Work Package Queue

Making a list of things to work on is commonly done whether it is a todo list or a full-fledged project plan. This practice differs in three significant ways.

First, the list is put into priority order. The order is based on some criteria that you identify that tells which things are most important (top of the queue) and which are least important (bottom of the queue). We call it a queue to remind us that there is an order to the list; you do the first thing first, then the next thing and so on.

Second, the queue is continuously maintained. You do not just make a queue of work then start at the top and work your way to the bottom. This works fine in situations where nothing changes, but if what you want is greater business agility then you need new practices to allow for possibly frequent change. So, you review the queue regularly and make changes to it as needed based on your current understanding.

Finally, the work on the queue is described in a set of relatively small, nearly independent, testable work packages. These topics are discussed in greater detail below.

The benefits you will get for this practice include greater flexibility in when you deliver results, being able to distribute work anywhere in the world while maintaining quality and schedules, and providing an effective means of increasing staff on a particular effort without incurring the negative consequences described by Brook's Law. *

---

* Fred Brooks in "The Mythical Man-Month" said that "adding manpower to a late software project makes it later". Experience shows this is not always true.

Work Packages

Work packages are not a new concept, but they are not well-understood today. The definition has been so simplified over the years that it is essentially meaningless. The PMI current definition of a work package is "the lowest level of a WBS (work breakdown structure)."

The most important part of the description of a work package, independence, has been lost over time. This is unfortunate, because being able to divide work into independent, well-defined work packages makes solution development far easier, more responsive to users, of higher quality, and reportable to management in a meaningful way. Doing a poor job defining work packages creates a complicated mess.

A work package is a description of a relatively small, nearly independent, testable piece of work. A work package will have a brief description, an estimate of effort (which gives you schedule and budget), and deliverables. Work packages can be described using items such as a use case, user story, service request, defect report, report mockup, screen mockup, workflow, feature, or component. Done well, you can assign work packages to individuals or teams working independently without creating dependencies between teams.

If your managers divide the work into work packages, and then produce a dependency diagram and one or more critical paths for the work packages, the work packages are not independent. The whole point of a work package is they do not have dependencies of any kind (including ordering by time). Done correctly, there is no critical path for work packages because there are no dependencies. There are often cases where you cannot achieve the ideal, but dependencies between work packages should always be minimized.

Any particular work package is relatively small (typically can be completed in less than 4 weeks and often in just a few days), well-defined (can be estimated and tested), able to be assigned to any team, valuable (to the business/users/company), and can ideally be able to be removed from the schedule without impacting other work. This last is

> **Example 1 Work Packages - Visiting Friends in St. Louis, Missouri**
> - Ride to the top of the Gateway Arch
> - Ride a paddle wheel boat
> - See a ball game at the Stadium
> - Visit the St. Louis Zoo
> - Go to a performance of the St. Louis Symphony Orchestra
> - Visit the Botanical Gardens
>
> **Example 2 Work Packages - Maintain my House**
> - Fix the driveway
> - Repair the roof
> - Landscape the backyard
> - Update the appliances in the kitchen
> - Modernize the master bathroom
> - Replace the second floor carpeting

sometimes not possible, but it is the goal we are working toward because that provides the greatest flexibility and overall efficiency.

Let us look at examples of work packages from real life. Example one is visiting friends in St. Louis, Missouri and example two is maintaining a house you own.

These are all good work packages. Each one is independent of the others, and could be done or not without effecting other work packages. With a little more detail as to what is involved in each one, each work package could have its own budget and amount of time. Different people could implement the work packages independently.

Even when visiting friends, everyone does not have to do everything all together. So for example some people could go to the zoo while others visit the botanical gardens. And clearly each work package for the house could be done by different teams of people.

In the example of the house, some of the work packages are actually larger than we would like, so over time each one would be decomposed into smaller work packages. The work packages that are probably too large are landscape the backyard, update the appliances, and modernize the bathroom. If you were doing this work at your home, you would almost certainly divide this kind of work into smaller pieces, such as replacing one appliance at a time or landscaping the backyard in sections.

Queues

A queue is an ordered list. When you put items on a queue, something is first, something else is second and so on. Formally or not, you have some criteria for deciding the order of items on the queue. Dependency is one way to order things. Without critical paths we need a different way to determine what is done first, second, and so on.

Often the criteria come from the definition of success. You can find these criteria by completing a statement such as "You know the current work on the product is successful when _____". It might be that the users are thrilled with the new features so you get a lot of new sales. It might be that a really annoying bug is fixed so you get good online comments from users. It might be that you get a feature to market before competitors do. Whatever your reason, identifying these criteria can help you organize the work packages on the queue.

Other times criteria come from risk mitigation strategies. There may be a risk that some new technology does not perform as expected so you will be unable to deliver as you planned. A work package to test and report on the new technology might be prioritized before anything else because the outcome of that work package will determine what you can or cannot do.

Note this approach does not create dependencies between work packages because the later work packages are not yet defined. In fact, this is a very agile approach to creating work packages; do not try to describe all the work up front, but plan to test first, then based on what you learn, describe the additional work that needs to be done. It may be that the outcome of your test is to do no additional work in that area.

Different criteria can completely change the order of the work

Example 1 Work Packages - Visiting Friends in St. Louis, Missouri
Criteria: Pleasant weather conditions
- Visit the St. Louis Zoo
- See a ball game at the Stadium
- Ride a paddle wheel boat
- Ride to the top of the Gateway Arch
- Visit the Botanical Gardens
- Go to a performance of the St. Louis Symphony Orchestra

Example 2 Work Packages - Maintain my House
Criteria: Long term upkeep
- Repair the roof
- Fix the driveway
- Replace the second floor carpeting
- Update the appliances in the kitchen
- Modernize the master bathroom
- Landscape the backyard

packages on your queue. Think about the house example: the order of the work packages will be different if your criteria is long term upkeep versus a criteria of personal comfort. When visiting friends, the order of the work packages will be different for winter weather and summer weather.

It is good to state the criteria you use to put the queue in order so everyone understands why the work packages are organized the way they are. If the people implementing the work packages understand what is important to you, then they know what questions to ask or what solutions to offer when lower level decisions need to be made. If my house criteria is long term upkeep, then I would expect to be offered options such as replace the driveway and not just get bids to patch and seal (which is a better match for a criteria of lowest cost). Notice that the queues have been reordered from the original based on the stated criteria.

Continuously Maintained

In every project we have to have a means for dealing with change. Unless your work is incredibly short (measured in hours), then the chances of a change being needed at some point are quite high. The further out you plan, the greater the likelihood that something will have to be changed.

I once worked for four years on a project that lasted 17 years. In that 17 year period, the hardware changed, the operating system changed, what was technically possible changed, and what the customer wanted changed. We went from applications running on green screen terminals connected to mainframes to applications running on graphical user interfaces on workstations connected to UNIX back-end servers.

Those changes were rather extreme but they happened over a 17 year period. With the advent of mobile, our markets are changing almost that much in much shorter periods. In 2010, people were somewhat more likely to browse the internet through a browser than an app. In 2012, people were somewhat more likely to browse the internet through an app. In 2012, if you had to choose between building a mobile enabled web site or a mobile app, it was not always clear which was the better choice. In 2014, 80% of people are on the internet using apps on some kind of mobile device. In 2014, you have to have an app. That is a big market change in less than 5 years.

Frequent change can be more easily managed by continuously maintaining the queue of work packages rather than waiting for someone to request a change. Continuously maintained means we do not create the queue of work packages once and then work until the queue is empty. Rather, we create an initial set of work packages, then after some work packages are completed, we revisit the queue to determine if change is required. You may need to remove work packages, add new work packages, change the order of the work packages, or change the description, schedule, and/or budget of work packages. Instead of writing all the work packages once, now a manager has to actively manage the

Example 1 Work Packages - Visiting Friends in St. Louis, Missouri
Criteria: It is unpleasantly hot outside
- Go to a performance of the St. Louis Symphony Orchestra
- Ride to the top of the Gateway Arch
- Ride a paddle wheel boat
- Visit the Botanical Gardens
- See a ball game at the Stadium
- Visit the St. Louis Zoo

Example 2 Work Packages - Maintain my House
Criteria: Sell the house
- Repair the roof
- Fix the driveway
- Offer a home buyer warranty

queue of work over a period of time.

To avoid a lot of rework, we write the work packages as close to the time they will be implemented as we can. The longer the time it will be before the work package will be implemented, the less detail we include. That way, you only do the work of detailing a work package (market research, competitor analysis, interviews, estimating, budgeting, etc.) when you are sure you will be implementing the work package. The more likely some information will change, the longer you wait to make a decision.

At the same time, you have to detail the work packages far enough ahead to plan and get resources. We say that we want to make decisions "at the last responsible moment". Wait to detail the work packages until you have as complete information as is feasible, but do not wait so long that other people's work is delayed waiting for you to make a decision.

It may happen that your criteria change over time. When the criteria change, the queue changes as well. For the visiting friends example, you might initially order the queue based on the weather being nice. But when you arrive in St. Louis, it is miserably hot, so you change the order of the work packages on the queue to start with activities that include air conditioning. For your house, it may be that you get a great opportunity to move into a new home, and so you decide to sell your current house. Notice how the queues have changed based on the new criteria.

For the house, notice we added one work package and got rid of four more. They are no longer important when the criteria is get the house ready for sale, because they are all things the new owners will have personal preferences about. If we do the work, whatever is done could actually harm our ability to sell the house. (If it looks old, they will probably just plan to replace it. If it looks new and they do not like it, they probably will not make an offer.)

This example illustrates why we do not want to be locked into a plan and budget far in advance of the work. What if we had planned the work on the house a year in advance and signed non-cancellable contracts for the work? You would not do that in your personal life, you should not do that at work.

What is so Hard About This?

The hard part of implementing a continuously maintained prioritized queue of work is that someone has to be accountable for managing the queue of work packages. This includes creating the work packages, prioritizing the work packages, and updating the queue in response to change. Ideally this queue of work packages is independent of any project and is continuously maintained for the lifetime of an asset that you manage. In most companies, you will start by focusing on creating queues at a project level because creating a queue of work packages at an asset level is a big change with widespread impact (and therefore hard to implement).

Ideally, the person managing the queue is the Asset Steward* (Product Owner, Product Marketing Manager, Business Manager, or

---

* An Asset Steward is someone with fiduciary responsibility for one or more capital assets.

Process Owner might be other titles) for the asset, or some person with authority to whom the Asset Steward delegates the work. This delegate is often found in the role of a Marketing Engineer, Subject Matter Expert, or Business Analyst. The Asset Steward or their delegate is the right person to ensure that you are delivering the right product at the right time for the right ROI, because that is a responsibility of the Asset Steward. This is not the same role as a Sponsor of a Project. The person you are looking for is the person responsible for the long term vision of the asset.

Some companies have difficulty finding someone to be responsible for the queue because they have no such role within the company. There is no one responsible for the long term vision and ROI of a capital asset. If that is true at your company, the first place to implement this practice will be at the project level and the project Sponsor should be responsible for the queue of work for that project.

You may run into resistance from several parts of the organization if you do not describe all the work packages for a project up front. To avoid large impacts to the organization (difficult change), have your teams write all the work packages at the start of an effort (project, program, release cycle), with just enough detail to be able to estimate work effort for each one. Creating independent work packages has a lot of benefit because it makes balancing work across the company easier. For many projects, there will likely be very little change in work packages throughout the project, so traditional change control processes are sufficient.

The skill of dividing work into relatively small, mostly independent, testable work packages is not common today. People are not trained in it from either a business or technology perspective. Most of your people will need training and coaching in how to do this. Some will have had training, and some just naturally do it from innate skill. But for most people, this is a knowledge gap that will have to be bridged.

A lot of your company's project management problems have a root cause of poorly created work packages, so creating good work packages helps all projects, not just Agile. If you don't think you have project management problems then either they are being hidden from you or you are choosing to fool yourself. Poor project management practices are rampant in companies of all sizes.

What are the Benefits of the Practice?

This practice is particularly useful in situations where the people maintaining and enhancing your assets are in different geographical locations or even work for different companies. This one practice will make teams with distributed members (such as offshore staff augmentation or work at home) function much better. Even when everyone is in the same place, if there are multiple teams of people working on the project, you get great benefit.

You gain several benefits in terms of cost and time. If your teams do a good job of describing the deliverables to the work packages, and they deliver what was described, you will have greatly reduced errors due to miscommunication. If the work packages are created in such a way as to be independent, you no longer have delays where one team is waiting for another to complete their work. You greatly reduce time spent in coordination meetings, which means more time is spent developing the solution.

There are also benefits to management. Work packages provide you greater flexibility in assigning work. Since the work packages are independent, you can assign them to anyone available world wide (your people, vendors, contractors, outsource shops, etc.). You have an option to deliver faster by having multiple teams work in parallel. It is often possible to change work packages that are not yet implemented with very little impact on the implementation teams.

I once was asked to mentor a program that was made up of two highly interconnected projects. I worked closely with management to examine all the requirements of the two projects as if they were one. We then divided the work into a different set of five independent projects with well-defined interfaces based on a common data architecture and workflow. The original two projects were to be delivered within three years after I started working with them. Instead, the five projects were run in parallel and the whole effort completed in one year. Because the projects were independent of each other, management had a choice whether to run them in sequence (as originally planned) or to run them all at the same time, thus delivering sooner.

Benefit to the Individual

If a person wants to create a prioritized queue of work packages for his/her own work, it is very easy to put this in place because the person can do it on their own without needing anyone else to be involved.

Doing this practice gives a person the confidence to always know what to work on next. It allows a person to focus on one work package to completion, which is far more efficient than multitasking. Making each work package independent enables faster delivery of the work to testers or users.

Benefit to the Project

If a project manager wants to create a prioritized queue of work packages for the project, this is relatively easy to do. The Project Manager can do it for the planning work but has to convince the tech lead and other implementers to be sure their work is described in work packages and added to the queue.

The benefit to the project is that the impact of change is much easier to determine because all the work packages are already prioritized on a queue. The project manager can see exactly what is impacted and how important that work is. Because of the independence of work packages, it is also much easier to adjust to changes late in the project, to balance work loads among multiple teams, to scale staff up or down as needed, and to shorten the project schedule by doing more work in parallel.

Benefit to the Asset

If an Asset Steward wants to create a prioritized queue of work packages for an asset, that is easy to do, and when those work packages are used to describe scope items, then there is no real change to the portfolio process. If IT is pushing for this change, then they have to convince the Asset Steward that this is a good idea. If there is no one in a role of Asset Steward (or Asset Steward delegate) then you have no one to do this work, and now you have to convince the business side to create such a role (which if you want business agility you want to do anyway).

Maintaining a prioritized queue of independent work packages makes it much easier for an Asset Steward to quickly adjust to changes in the market. If the work packages are approved once a year, there will still be the effort to make change requests unless the portfolio process changes as well. Because this queue allows an Asset Steward to continuously stream work to an implementation team, any change to the queue should have almost no impact on the work of the implementation team (note this is only true if work packages are independent).

Benefit to the Portfolio

At many large companies the description of work at the portfolio level is much too detailed and inflexible. I have been shocked to find C-level executives in multi-billion dollar companies tracking how $1 million is being spent. This is less than 0.1% of what the company spends. This is equivalent to someone with $1000 deciding how to spend one penny or less. Is this really the best use of time for someone that senior in the company? Decisions about something that small should be made by someone lower in the organization.

Instead of a portfolio made up of work packages, the portfolio should be based on goals, metrics to measure progress toward those goals, and perhaps a few really large initiatives as needed. Different areas of the company receive funding to determine and implement solutions to meet the goals. Solutions are not decided by the portfolio team. Keeping back some money to handle contingencies throughout the year provides the portfolio team flexibility to adjust spending throughout the year.

Giving someone a budget and pushing decision making down to the person on the spot at the time the decision has to be made allows for much greater business agility than trying to describe all the projects to be done in the next year. At the same time, people do have to be held accountable for how they manage the budget they are allocated. Those people will describe the work needed to maintain and enhance an asset in work packages. The portfolio team can receive much more accurate ROI and progress metrics when these are based on work packages.

How to Get Started

To start implementing this practice, find an Asset Steward (probably a Product Manager) who wants to control the implementation of his or her asset. Sadly, not every Asset Steward thinks this is a responsibility of the role, and some Asset Stewards will abandon their asset responsibilities to those who are implementing the solution. Do not try to fight this fight up front; prove benefit first with those who want to truly manage their asset and let their successes drive change in more resistant parts of your company. If you have an asset in a fast changing market, your Asset Steward for that asset will most likely be delighted with this practice.

If you cannot find an Asset Steward to work with, start with Project Managers. They are not as close to the users as Asset Stewards, nor do they have responsibility for the long term vision of the asset, so you may not improve the delivery of a better asset to the users, but you will see higher quality and reduced cost and time for projects that create queues of work packages and manage them. If the work packages are truly independent pieces of work with well-defined deliverables, then you remove most of the need for teams to coordinate, you remove delays due to dependencies on missed deliverables, and you have greatly reduced errors due to miscommunication.

Chapter 2

Regular Demonstrations of Functional Solutions

Project status reports are a common tool for managers at all levels to understand the progress of a project. They are also commonly known to not really do the job, as recognized by the statement "90% complete, 90% left to do". The problem is that knowledge work is typically impossible to predict just how long it will take.

Leonard Cohen spent over 5 years composing his very popular song "Hallelujah" (you heard it in Shrek just after Shrek and Fiona had a fight and she leaves to marry Lord Farquaad). This is an extremely popular song, covered by a lot of artists. Contrast this with Bob Dylan claiming that he wrote the song "I and I" in 15 minutes. If you had asked before they started how long it would take to compose a song the question probably would not make sense to them. They would probably answer that takes what it takes.

The point is that until the product has been completed, whether a song, book, software, or any other kind of knowledge product, no one can really accurately predict how much is left to do. The person or people producing the work may have a "feeling" for how long it will take, but may be surprised by a flash of insight that makes the work go much faster, or find they need a long period of test and learn which slows the work down. To overcome the problem of not being able to estimate the work, this practice says we show progress by regularly demonstrating a working solution. When you see something working, there is no guess about how complete the work is.

The benefits to this practice are that you always know exactly how much is complete, you can get feedback from users well before the end of the project, the team does not have the time to procrastinate the start of the work, and in general the implementation team is happier about their work because you have set your teams up with a habit of success. Projects using this practice are far more likely to be delivered on time with a solution that is well received by the users.

Functional Solution

A functional solution is one that is completed, tested, and it works. It may be only part of what you will eventually need, but that one part is complete. Remember work packages? They make a good unit of functional solution – relatively small, nearly independent, with a description of what done means, a work package can be completely implemented and tested to show that it works as defined.

Many people have the mistaken impression that if something is a functional solution, this means it is everything we need to release to users. That is not the case at all. We must distinguish between having a work package that works, is complete, and tested and having a complete solution ready for users. Some things are quick to develop, but others will take a lot of time. We can still show intermediate progress with working solutions.

I have worked on software that took anywhere from 4 weeks to 4 years (and more) to develop a complete solution that was delivered to real users. With all my code, every day I completed and tested at least one thing that I could (if asked) demonstrate that it worked. Every day. So when someone tells me they cannot possibly deliver something functional and tested in less than 10 weeks, I just do not believe it. The issue is not one of programming (or other creative) skill. It is an issue of learning how to decompose the work.

Sometimes your implementation team does not want to deliver completely functional parts of the solution because they think it takes too much time to get the partial solution to that level of completeness and they feel they should spend that time on developing more of the solution. In order to show something works, the team may be required to develop stubs or frameworks that will be replaced over time with the "real solution". The team sees this as a waste, and from the perspective of creating code that is meant to be replaced, it is a waste. That misses the point.

The point of this practice is that until you have a working solution (even if partial) you do not really know what it will take to develop that solution, nor do you really know if it is correct. We are solving the problem of having a correct solution, not the problem of eliminating rework. (Rework can be a very good thing, so a later topic will discuss when rework is good and when it is not. You do not actually want a goal of eliminating all rework; it will cause you long term problems.) The time spent in making the partial solution demonstrable is more than made up by finding and fixing problems much earlier in the process.

Consider our example of maintaining the house. You might try one kind of patch on part of the driveway and maybe a different kind of patch on another part of the driveway to see which works better before deciding which approach to use on the whole driveway. You might even decide that patching is not going to do the job and instead you will replace the driveway. You quickly find out the best approach at small expense and make the decision when you have complete information. When you need to test and learn (and most of the time when people are the users you do) then dividing the work into small demonstrable chunks lets you go faster overall.

Regular Demonstrations

Test cases tell us if the solution works as described – did we create the solution correctly. Demonstrations to human beings tell us if we are creating the right solution.

It is extremely difficult for a person to imagine something he or she wants and to describe it completely and correctly such that another person can create it. This is why we see the use of sketches, prototypes, mockups, miniatures, and early creation of partial solutions in most fields of endeavor, especially those involving physical product.

A building designer creates detailed architectural drawings, and may include samples of flooring, window coverings, and paint color chips to help the builder know what to do. A sculptor creating a commissioned work of art creates a mini model of what she will sculpt to show her client to be sure the art is what they expect, then uses the miniature for reference when creating the final piece. A set designer for a stage show creates a miniature scale model of all the sets on a scale model of the stage to be sure everything works together, and the set builders use the model as a reference as they are building the sets.

This approach is just as good for knowledge workers. An author sending a book proposal has to include a table of contents and one or more complete chapters to the publisher for consideration before a contract will be signed. A good software architect will write small amounts of code for different possible solutions before selecting one. What is inside of someone's head cannot be evaluated. How do you know the implementation team is creating what you want? You know by seeing it.

Most software projects have a time at the end for user acceptance testing for exactly the purpose of verifying that the right solution was created. But that is very late to find out the team got it wrong. There is very little, if any, time and money left to fix any problems discovered. Instead, demonstrate parts of the solution regularly so you do have time to fix any problems that are discovered.

Regular demonstrations happen on a regular schedule such as every two weeks or every three weeks. The actual schedule will depend on the nature of the work. Having a rhythm makes it easier to schedule – just put it in the calendar for every three weeks. People grow to expect the demo and actually feel that something is wrong if they miss it. They can schedule planned time off, other meetings, or other deliverables around something that happens on a regular schedule.

In the demonstration, the team who is implementing the solution shows the work they have completed and tested since the last demonstration. The key is the solution has to be usable. If it is a business process, you can do the process and get the expected results. If it is software, you can run it to see how it works. If it is a scale model in preparation for full production, you can touch it and move the parts. If it is firmware, and the hardware is not yet available, you can run it in an IDE or simulator. If you are planning for a trade show, you have an actual booth set up to walk in and around.

The people attending the demo should be actual users if at all possible. You should also invite any stakeholders of the work and the team's manager. Some companies advertise their demos internally, and anyone interested can attend. Sometimes teams working on related efforts want to attend to know exactly what is being developed and to get a better idea of where they may be able to collaborate on the solution or coordinate efforts.

In our examples, we can demonstrate success. We can visit the St. Louis Symphony and prove it by showing ticket stubs and pictures of us at Symphony Hall. We can go to an exhibit at the St. Louis Zoo and based on that experience, decide if we want to continue seeing the animals at the zoo or do something else. We can make one patch on the driveway and examine it before committing to the whole job. Or perhaps we visit an installation of a new driveway, examine it, and talk with the owners before deciding to replace the driveway. The important thing is that we experience some part of the solution, and based on what we learn through that experience, we make decisions about the best approach.

What is so Hard About This?

Initially, your implementation team may not want to do this. They are challenged to have something working sooner than they want. They think they are wasting time showing the work when they could be implementing the solution. But the first time they get feedback on their work – this is great, this needs some fixing, you are missing something here – they are sold on the approach and want to keep doing it.

The other people who do not want to do this are the audience for the demo. It seems unnecessary, it is hard to schedule with many busy people, and the solution will be delivered anyway. The first time your audience gets to provide feedback and the team responds to it, your audience will love the idea.

Now over time, especially if executives are involved, they may want to decrease the number of demos. At one company I worked for, an Agile software team working on an eight month project was doing a great job of demonstrating working production quality software every three weeks. For the first three months, the executive sponsor and stakeholders were happy to come to every demo. But things were going really well, so they asked to come every other demo. After missing one demo, the executive sponsor and stakeholders started worrying about the project. They started calling the project manager asking how it was going. He pointed out to them that they would know how the project was going if they had attended the demo. They never missed another demo for the rest of the project because the regular feedback was that important to them. They believed what they saw with their own eyes more than they believed a status report.

Sometimes high level executives think these demos are a waste of time and want their managers to stop doing them. That is because they are not personally involved and do not personally benefit from the practice. Try inviting some high level executives to some demos to observe what happens when the implementation team meets with users, stakeholders, and management to get their feedback on the actual working solution.

What are the Benefits of the Practice?

A big technical benefit is that the team finds errors (especially requirements errors) early when it is easiest and least expensive to fix them. Finding a requirements error early may cost X to fix. Finding the same error during final testing before releasing to production can cost 100X to fix. Finding the error after delivery to users has been shown to cost as much as 1000X to fix.

Every team of implementers I know who have tried this love the results. They get early feedback about whether or not they are on the right track which prevents them from putting a lot of time into the wrong thing. We almost always find something not quite right at these demonstrations. Most of the time it is a little thing. Sometimes the team had a huge misunderstanding and they have to start over. But they start over having invested a small amount of time into the work rather than finding out at the end that what they have is wrong.

You get a better product by regularly demonstrating a functional solution. This is the most powerful thing you can do to produce product that better meets the user needs, with higher quality, lower cost, and on schedule. The insights gained by everyone concerned – the implementation team, their managers, other stakeholders, users – are so valuable that once the habit is established no one will want to stop doing this practice.

From a management point of view, this practice will tell you the actual progress of the project. You can see exactly what is complete and what is not. This is very different from a typical status report. You see your product working with your own eyes. Lack of progress cannot be hidden behind percentages and statistics. If you convince the managers to invite real users and listen to their feedback, this practice provides eye-opening insights. Asset Stewards have traditionally run Beta programs with select customers for exactly this purpose. We just want to do it more often than once at the end. In this digital age, it is easier than ever to get feedback from real users.

A final benefit is that the team can profit from lessons learned and apply those lessons throughout the project, instead of finding at delivery that they have been making the same mistake over and over.

One team I mentored had what I consider a very successful demo. They worked for 2 weeks on a report needed by a manager in their area, the first one of many. When they showed the report, the manager rejected it. The data was correct, but because of the way the report was laid out, it was confusing and unusable. The team realized they should have created an initial paper mockup of the report instead of just collecting what data was needed. The problem was found early, could be easily corrected at that time, and led the team to adopt a practice of creating mockups that would make their later work much more likely to be correct the first time.

Benefit to the Individual

A member of the implementation team benefits from the demonstration because he or she knows as soon as possible if the work is correct or not. When it is correct, there is a glow of satisfaction for a job well done. When it is not correct, there is time to fix the problem well before the end of the project, which removes the stress of working to fix problems at the last minute.

Benefit to the Project

The project benefits because there are almost never problems found late, and when they are, the problems are almost always small and easily fixed. The project is much more likely to deliver the solution that is needed on time and on budget. In addition, it is very easy to determine progress based on work that is fully complete and deliverable.

Benefit to the Asset

The asset benefits from frequent feedback because we are much more likely to deliver what the users actually want. This helps us make more sales, increase customer satisfaction, and beat competitors.

Benefit to the Portfolio

Regular demonstrations of progress are the best proof of status. The portfolio team knows exactly what has been completed and how much of the schedule and budget were spent to get to that point. They also know if the work to date is valuable based on the feedback collected at the demonstration. This allows the portfolio team to make decisions about whether to supply additional funding for the project if it is requested. The portfolio team also has much greater visibility into how money is being spent.

How to Get Started

The key is to plan ahead. The implementation team will be quite unhappy if someone just shows up one day asking for a demonstration of progress. They have to interrupt what they are doing to do the demonstration and they may not be at a point where a demonstration is feasible. Those who will view the demonstration need to find out from the implementation team what will be shown and when so that expectations are managed on all sides.

Sometimes you just have to insist to the implementation team that they have to do demonstrations of progress. So far, every team I have convinced to do demos complained about the first one, but loved doing it ever time after that, because they themselves benefitted from the feedback provided by those viewing the demonstration.

The implementation team will ask what to do if they are not ready. The answer is they should show what is complete and be honest about what is not complete. The demonstration pushes the team to see that they are either 100% done or not done. This is a more honest appraisal of progress. What is important is what we can deliver today, not what we might be able to sell in a few months of work. It makes the implementation team more aware of the market drivers for the company.

Chapter 3

Incremental Delivery of Solution

A review of large software projects in the 1960's revealed that every project would benefit from being planned as two increments. Those projects that tried to do just one increment found they had to do a follow-up project to fix the problems they did not have the time to fix in the original project. Our projects that deliver the solutions we need to stay in business are much more complex today than they were then. Interesting, I was told exactly the same thing about the need for follow-up projects at a large internationally well-known company just a few weeks ago. And I have heard it continuously throughout my career in the Fortune 200.

Incremental delivery of solution formalizes what we all know in practice we need to do by suggesting we plan a minimum of two increments of any except the tiniest projects. The longer the effort, the more increments should be planned. For example, a one year project might have 3 or 4 increments. For projects concerning work in fast changing markets, you want many short increments to provide greater flexibility to keep up with market change. These increments might be 2-3 weeks in length.

The benefits to this practice include getting feedback well before the end of the project when there is still time to fix problems, delivering a solution that better meets user needs, and completing the work without having to schedule a follow-up project.

Incremental Delivery

In a traditional project structure, all the project work is completed and then the results are made available to users once at the end of the project. Already by the late 1960's, when software systems were becoming complex, this approach was determined to be flawed. This is because it turns out to be impossible to get everything right up front. Our products are so complex, the needs of the users are so broad, that no matter how hard we try, we will miss something, make some mistake. Today, the products we create are far more complex than those created in the 1960's, and so the problem is even larger.

No matter how the implementation teams work, whether they use Waterfall, Kanban, Scrum, Rational Unified Process, or any other software development lifecycle, you want to plan for multiple releases or deliveries of the solution. How many you plan is largely a factor of the how much is unknown. The more unprecedented the work, the more releases you should plan in order to find the mistakes you have certainly made as soon as possible when you have time to fix them.

This is called incremental delivery because we are releasing the solution in increments. Each increment includes a subset of the solution that is functionally complete with the expectation that this increment is finished (unless of course we find problems that have to be fixed). This is different from iterative where the part of the solution that is complete is finished from the point of view of testing and validation, but may not yet have complete functionality. There is an expectation in iterative development that we may need to continue to evolve this part of the solution until it has all of the intended functionality.

Imagine you are going to draw a picture. One way to do it is to divide your piece of paper into squares and draw the part of the picture that appears in one square completely. It would have outline, colors, and shading. Then you draw the next square. This is what incremental delivery is like. One square is one increment of the solution.

Now change the approach. This time when you draw the picture you outline the entire picture. Then you add color to the entire picture, and finally you do the shading for the entire picture. That is what iterative delivery is like. One iteration is the drawing, the second is the coloring, and the third is the shading.

One multi-country project I worked with planned to develop the solution over a period of four years and release everything to users at the end. I convinced the managers to plan a series of incremental releases, with the actual users doing the acceptance tests. They had already been working on requirements for a year and were not sure they needed more information, but planning multiple increments seemed less risky than waiting three more years to find out if the users liked the product. They planned the first release for 9 months later. The users did acceptance testing and everyone involved discovered there had been some significant misunderstandings of user needs. Because they had actual product to work with, the users could demonstrate exactly what they expected and the results they actually got. This was such useful information that the implementation team committed to scheduling more intermediate releases on a shorter schedule so they could get the feedback sooner.

It is important to note that these incremental releases were not released to the general public until the actual end of the project. But the incremental releases were released to a subset of the user community who did have the product installed on their own machines to use during the day at their jobs to continue to provide feedback to the project team. This is very much like the idea of an alpha release, beta release, and so on before a product is released to market. The difference is we plan a number of these cycles throughout the project, not one at the end.

In the examples of friends visiting us, it is very easy to see that the vacation plans are incremental. Going to the zoo is one increment. Going to the symphony is another increment. With the example of the house, if we have a house and garage that both need the roof replaced, we might do an increment of the garage first to see how the new roof turns out, or see if we like working with the contractor, before doing the roof on the house. Depending on the cost, we might have the house roof replaced in increments to spread the cost out over a longer period. In my current house, we are planning to install solar panels on the roof. But the roof is getting very old and will need replacing within 5 years. When we replace the roof, we will have to remove the solar panels then reinstall them. Do we replace the whole roof now, or replace an increment now, the part that will be under the solar panels, then replace the rest later?

Capitalization versus Expense

Some companies have difficulty with many short releases because of their need to capitalize work. When a product is made generally available to customers that is the point in time when the work on that product is capitalized. If the amount of work that was done since the last release is too small, it cannot be capitalized and instead must be expensed.

The finance people will know that there are significant differences between these two approaches. Capitalized work on a product increases the value of that product (which is now a capital asset) in the company accounting books. Capital assets have a real value and can be used for purposes such as securing loans. Work that is expensed does not increase the value of a capital asset.

Short iterations have a lot of value in terms of finding problems as early as we possibly can. You can get the benefit without releasing that iteration for general availability. This has long been a practice at many companies that release an iteration of a product to a limited number of users in order to solicit feedback. A set of iterations can be kept in a holding area until there is enough new work completed that it can be capitalized. At that point the product is made generally available and the work is capitalized. This allows you to get the benefit of short increments or iterations and still be able to capitalize the work.

What is so Hard About This?

Incremental development is naturally a part of most software development lifecycles because it is so very effective at finding problems early and keeping long projects on track to deliver on time and on budget. Even Waterfall projects are recommended to have at least two increments.

Many people do not want to do incremental Waterfall because they think it will take more time and delay project completion. Those who try incremental delivery quickly find that the extra time they spend per increment is easily made up later in the project with a solution that is easier to integrate with few-to-no late serious errors to fix at the very end.

If you are doing incremental delivery of a Waterfall project, you may have to repeat some phase gates multiple times. Ideally, the Waterfall project will start with an early discovery phase where the high level requirements and architecture are described. Then in each increment, there is a detailed requirements and design phase which will likely require review and sign off before the implementation work can begin. While there are more of these review sessions (one per increment) each one should be much shorter than doing a large, perhaps multi-week, review up-front. It is also much more likely that the reviews will be more effective simply because there is less information to absorb at a time.

With incremental delivery, planning for the use of people in different roles may be more challenging. Instead of needing the Business Analyst to do requirements for just a month or two at the start of a large effort, now you need less time at the beginning but you also need that person's time periodically throughout the project, at the start of each increment. The rhythm of the project changes and so in a matrix organization every manager has to be aware of the new rhythm in order to staff the projects appropriately. This can be a big challenge for projects that want to do many increments, such as Agile projects.

What are the Benefits of the Practice?

With incremental delivery, at all times you know exactly what is completed – ready for market – and what is not. You can make decisions to extend deadlines or release with reduced feature sets based on actual completed work. You know when there are problems that need to be addressed early when it is easiest and least expensive to fix those problems. You know when it is time to cancel work that is not going well, thus saving time and money for other things.

Your implementation teams get into a habit of success. It just feels good to finish something. Then you do it again and again. This leads to what Menlo Innovations CEO Richard Sheridan calls a joyful workplace. (See his book "Joy, Inc." which describes how he built Menlo Innovations into a joyous place to work and the advantages he has found from that.) You have invested money in your people. Keeping them happy at work is much less expensive than having them quit and you have to reinvest in someone new.

Research has also found that projects of 6 months or less are much more likely to complete on time and budget than longer projects. Creating a series of increments for large efforts, each of which is 6 months long or less, gives the same benefits as short projects. Each increment is planned and estimated on its own, the team has a relatively short schedule to meet, so motivation is high and procrastination is low.

Benefit to the Individual

Getting something finished feels good. Everyone likes to know they have completed a job and that it was well-done. Knowing that someone else is using your solution is a big satisfaction point for knowledge workers. Those good feelings make work much more delightful, and happy employees do better work.

Benefit to the Project

Decades of research shows us that unless the project is quite small, you will almost certainly need at least 2 increments to get it right. I know many, many companies that follow every project with a fix-it project or a continuous improvement project. These second projects are really the second increment. Planning 2 or more increments per project means you won't have to have a follow on project to fix the things you ran out of time to fix the first time around. This is better because when the project ends it really is complete and ready to deliver to users, instead of completing the first project and not being able to deliver it because it does not work until you have scheduled and completed the second project.

Benefit to the Asset

Releasing some of the features earlier will almost certainly make the users happy, and provides an opportunity for them to give you feedback when there is still time to do something about it. If this is a product you are selling, then releasing something earlier means you can start benefiting from sales of those new features earlier than the end of the project. This may also enable you to get a jump on the competition.

If you determine after the first increment that you don't need to do the rest of the planned work, you can easily cancel the succeeding increments and use the money saved to fund implementation of things that are more important. Since you did complete releasable work in the first increment, you have not wasted money as you would have in a pure Waterfall project. You have something delivered to show for your initial investment.

Benefit to the Portfolio

The benefits to the portfolio are the same as the benefits to the asset, but multiplied across all the assets in your company.

How to Get Started

Find a Project Manager of a Waterfall project who is willing to try the experiment. Ask the Project Manager to start by planning two increments for the project. More can be planned in later projects, but two is a good place to start for those not used to the approach. This is also a much easier change for the matrix managers than planning 6 or 8 increments. Start with two increments, let everyone have time to adjust to the new project rhythm, then try more increments in later projects.

The project plan will start with an early phase for high level requirements and architecture, followed by two complete increments.

Inside each increment will be a time for detailed requirements and design, review and signoffs if required, then implementation and testing, followed by user acceptance testing. Each increment may end with a release to market, or may be an internal or limited release to get feedback. After the second increment, a final integration and release phase may be planned to deliver everything to market (if each increment does not end with a release).

The project manager should review the work to be completed with the project sponsor and project architects to determine what work will be done first and what will be done second. Earlier work should be of high value to the business or users. Earlier work should also mitigate areas of high risk. The second increment should have less work planned than the first increment to allow time to incorporate lessons learned and feedback into the second increment.

Section Two

The Big Five Engineering Practices

At Stanford, we teach 'design thinking' - that is, we put together small, interdisciplinary groups to figure out what the true needs are and then to apply the art of engineering to serve them.

- *Hasso Plattner*

An Introduction to the Practices

The practices described in this section for the most part pre-date Agile by several decades. They were developed to improve the practice of software development in the same environment we see in most large corporations today: large initiatives with a distributed workforce where people are not dedicated to one effort at a time. While these practices are traditionally considered software engineering practices, many of them can be applied to any product. These practices are:

1. Architecture and Vision
2. Design by Contract
3. Refactoring
4. Quality Practices
5. Frameworks, Stubs, and Mock Objects

The practices in this section can be done by implementation teams with very little impact on the rest of the company. Changes in other parts of the company will make these practices even more effective, but if those other changes cannot be made, there are still advantages to adopting these practices even by individuals or teams. I have used these practices throughout my career in areas as diverse as programming a computer, structuring a business, launching a new product, creating a course, directing musicals, and even in writing this book.

No implementer should have to ask their manager if they can do these practices because they are all part of what the implementer should already be doing. These practices are often not done because management pushes for deadlines that are too short to do the work properly. The gain is in the short term (my project is cheaper), but the cost is huge over the long term as the product becomes harder and harder to change or fix. The increasing difficulty of change also prevents business agility. A company cannot be responsive to its market when it takes 6 months to make a change.

I have seen this over and over in large established companies: a change as simple as adding a field to a form costs $100,000 or more and takes at least 3 months. No one is surprised by this because it has become standard. Contrast that with Facebook being able to do the same change in no more than a week (according to a senior engineer I spoke to at that company). The difference is almost completely due to how the product is structured under the covers. The product called Facebook is structured in such a way that it is easy to update or change.

If you are the executive responsible for product delivery, then it is within your sphere of influence to institute practices to restructure your products so they are easier to change. Making your products easier to change enables business agility because when the business asks for a change we can do it quickly. If you are outside product delivery, your challenge will be to convince the executive in charge of product delivery to have her teams implement these changes.

One big reason for implementing the practices in this section is to reduce the cost of product development. This enables the implementation teams to do more with the same amount of money. Another big reason for implementing the practices in this section is to be able to respond more quickly to market changes. Some of your products may not be changing very quickly at all, and so this is not as important. In other cases, your products are losing market share to competitors because you cannot match or exceed the features or benefits they offer in time to retain your current customers, much less gain new ones.

Agile practices will let you move fast and for less money, but only if your product is structured "under the covers" in such a way that allows for this. This is probably the biggest unspoken issue around adopting

Agile in large established companies. People talk about culture, but a much bigger issue is how your products are structured, especially the software. This is a fundamental reason that large established companies are not seeing the Agile gains that are seen in small, new companies. The small, new companies in general have not been around long enough for their products to get to the size, complexity, or poor structuring that cause it to take 6 months to add a field to a form.

Instituting the practices in this section will not change things over night. Depending on how poorly the product is structured today, it might take 1-3 years (or longer) to get it restructured to the point where you see cost savings and faster time to market. Remember, your teams have to get their "real work" done while fixing the current product. There will be an upfront cost to fixing the problems; the advantages come later.

At the very least, any new development should be done using these practices to avoid having your new products end up in the same mess your current products are in. You may decide it is not worth the money to fix products that are approaching end-of-life or those that change infrequently.

I know of a very large European defense industry company that decided to restructure their primary product using the practices in this section along with incremental delivery and a strong focus on reuse. They had a 5 year plan to cut costs. The first 2 years, it cost about 10% more to develop their products because of needing to fix the existing problems as well as release new features. The third year they broke even, making up enough in that year to pay for the increased cost the previous 2 years. The fifth year they were priced at 85% of the lowest competitor with a much superior product and had a far higher profit margin than they ever had before. In general, to add features to the restructured product cost them about 55% of what they were previously spending.

Unfortunately the case study is no longer available. I guess no one wants to hear that these practices worked 20 years ago, or maybe they just don't want to hear that it was a 5 year effort to get this kind of gain.

Chapter 4

Architecture and Vision

Architecture describes the structure of something. Every product has an architecture, but not every product has a good architecture. A good architecture means it is easy to change or enhance your product for the kinds of changes or enhancements you anticipate making to the product as expressed in the product vision.

Not only should your product have a good architecture to start, but that architecture should be maintained over time or you lose the benefits of a good architecture. The architecture should always support the product vision, so it should evolve as the product vision evolves.

The benefits you get from having and evolving a good architecture are reduced lifetime cost of the product, a longer useful lifetime for the product, and greater business agility.

Architecture and Vision

A product needs a vision that tells what it is and where it is going. This includes the technology behind the product. How the product is put together, the architecture, should be designed in such a way to support the future likely business direction of the product.

If a small town builds a bridge over a river for mostly local traffic, they would be wise to construct it in such a way that it can be relatively easily expanded if the town grows to be large. There is no reason to build a large bridge now; they don't need it and the cost would be quite high. But knowing that cities tend to grow, planning and designing for expansion of the bridge is money well spent. This could be as simple as locating the bridge in a spot where another bridge could be built right next to it and the road on either side split so each bridge carries traffic one way. It costs almost no money today to allow for future expansion tomorrow.

You should consider your company's products in the same manner. How can we design the product today to allow for the planned future direction of the product? Or even further, how can we design the product today to allow for an unknown future direction? We can't account for everything, but some thought up front can save a lot of money later. These are the questions answered by a good architecture in alignment with the business vision.

Architecture is not specifically an Agile practice, but rather is an engineering practice. There have been architectures and architects as long as there has been engineering. Architecture in software predates Agile by more than 30 years. Many in the Agile community think that the practice of Architecture is not necessary, and yet few of them have been involved with very large long-lived companies who have been maintaining products for sometimes over 100 years and software products for more than 40 years. Mobile apps are small and likely to have lives measured in years. Some business applications are huge and have lives measured in decades. Architecture is not as important for mobile apps. Architecture is vital for applications that will have a long life.

I am not aware of any long-lived product that is flexible to change and easy to maintain that does not have a well-defined product architecture. Ultimately we are trying to be more agile as a business. We need our products to be flexible to change and easy to maintain so that we can respond quickly to changes in the market. A good architecture provides the structure that allows this business agility.

Ideally each of your products will have someone responsible for the business vision and someone responsible for the architecture that supports the business vision. For smaller products, the same people may be responsible for two or three small products, especially if some of them are slow changing so do not require much attention.

Many large companies coordinate the work of architects across products through an Enterprise Architecture group. This group includes architects of all disciplines: business, software, network, security, information & data, and user experience. This group is responsible for maintaining good architecture for each product and for the resources that are shared across products. While this sounds like a good idea, they can become a roadblock to progress. It is better to have the architects working in the implementation teams and create an architecture guild instead.

What is so Hard About This?

It is hard to convince people of the importance of architecture when the benefits and costs do not become apparent for many years. There have been few opportunities for direct comparisons between the same product with a good architecture and with a bad architecture.

Very few companies try to measure the goodness of their architectures, so do not know if their architecture is good or bad. We can determine this indirectly by the rising cost of maintaining a poorly architected product compared to the relatively flat cost of maintaining a well architected product. But there is typically not a consistent or accurate measure of the cost of a product over the years. Most companies focus on projects and programs, not products, so the information may be very hard to get to determine what the product actually costs over time.

Because this information is hard to find, many people would rather not believe it to be true. I have had people tell me I was wrong when I had actual data from their own company to show that bad architecture was costing a lot of money. Since the costs are not obvious and change is difficult, it is easy for an executive to ignore the issues. Likely that person will be rotated into a new job within a couple of years, far less time than it takes for the real costs to appear, so it is "not my problem".

Good architects are hard to find. The skill set requires being a big picture person who also pays attention to the details, someone who can think through all the things that can go wrong but also be an enthusiastic advocate, a great analyst who is also a great communicator. And on top of that, a good architect has a deep knowledge of the technical space your product is in. There are not a lot of good architects. The other problem is that it is hard to determine if someone really is a good architect or if the person is just a good salesperson who speaks well but cannot do the job. There are ways to test if a person is good at architecture, but they require the person doing the testing to be a good architect.

Good architects appear to be expensive when compared to programmers and many people think they are just senior programmers. No they are not senior programmers; architecture is a different skill set. A good architect will save you millions over the years. Companies like Facebook and Google, which were founded by geeks, put a lot of money into their architects and most senior engineers. They understand the long term value of these people and pay accordingly. Keep the conversation away from comparing pay between technical jobs, and focus on the value a good architect will bring to the product and the company.

Some people think that architecture is an overhead practice not directly contributing to the development of the product. These people want to reduce overhead and so get rid of (or resist hiring) architects. Since a good architect guides the development of the product through defining and maintaining the technical vision, this person is an integral part of the development of the product. Unfortunately the consequences of lack of architectural vision do not become evident for many years, long after the people who decided that having a person to maintain the architectural vision was not important have moved on to other jobs or retired.

In a company without an architecture practice, very likely technical leads have been making the decisions. They will not be happy if you ask them to give this up for a strong architectural practice because you are reducing their status in the organization. Some will have the talents needed to be architects and others will not.

You may have people fight this change for the rest of their careers at your company. I have seen this three times now in very large companies where one individual who was not chosen to be the architect for the product effectively stopped the entire transition. These people had convinced their managers that they were indispensable and the managers would do anything to keep them from quitting, including costing their companies millions of dollars in immediate documentable cost not to mention the long term problems they created. Do not fall into this trap; in a large company no one is indispensable. It may be painful to lose that person, but your company will not fail over it.

What are the Benefits of the Practice?

Without a strong business and technical vision of the product, changes and enhancements made by different teams could be done in ways that create inconsistencies and even failures in the product. You save money over time by not introducing those inconsistencies and failures. You also save money over time by thinking through today's and tomorrow's needs and choosing technology that supports both. I have many times seen a company purchase a solution or platform for a short term need, only to have to take the solution out and replace it when it could not handle the longer term needs. Many times this waste of time and money is avoidable.

When there is a clear business and technical vision of the product that is communicated to the teams who are implementing solutions, more decisions can be made by the teams without waiting for someone senior to figure it out. It seems a minor point, but much time can be wasted while a team waits for answers to sometimes very basic questions.

Products with a strong business and technical vision are typically better designed overall, which makes them easier (and therefore cheaper) to maintain over the long term. The cost difference can be huge, adding up to many millions of dollars over the lifetime of large, long lived products. Many long established companies are still selling products that were initially created when the company was founded, possibly over 100 years ago. Many long established companies today are running software that is over 40 years old.

With poorly architected software, the initial cost of software is approximately 2% of the total lifetime cost of that software. If that software cost $100,000 to create initially, this suggests that your company has spent over $5,000,000 to enhance and maintain that software over the years. Software that is better architected and maintained has an initial cost that is around 10% of the total lifetime cost. That would reduce your company's total lifetime cost to $1,000,000, for an 80% savings. I'm pretty sure your company spends a lot more than $100,000 a year developing software, so you can see that the cost savings can be quite significant.

Benefit to the Individual

Having a good architecture makes working on the product much easier. Changes can typically be made faster, and at the same time it is less likely for certain kinds of defects to be introduced.

Benefit to the Project

With a good architecture, updates to the product can be made faster and with higher quality.

Benefit to the Asset

In the long term, a product with a good architecture has a longer usable lifetime and has a lower lifetime cost of ownership. A well structured product gives you the opportunity for greater business agility.

Benefit to the Portfolio

With a suite of well-architected assets, less money is spent on maintaining those products over time, so there is more money available to develop new things.

How to Get Started

It is easiest to start when developing something new or making substantial changes to an existing product. In this case, before any implementation work is started, an architecture is created that supports the product vision both short-term and long-term.

For existing products, you will start by analyzing the current architecture to determine if making a change would make the product easier to maintain. Then you should analyze the cost of that change compared to the benefit. If the product is expected to be decommissioned in the next couple of years, then there may not be enough benefit to modifying the architecture to justify the cost.

A change to the architecture, even just a part of it, will involve refactoring the product and extensive testing to verify that nothing is broken. Sometimes it is better to plan to decommission the product and replace it with something new.

It is good to keep the architects on the implementation teams as their regular jobs, but at the same time there is work that the architects need to do together that goes across projects and products. To balance the needs, you may want to create an architecture guild. The guild is responsible for the practice of architecture at your company. All architects belong to the guild and participate in the work of the guild. It is not limited to a special group of senior architects or enterprise architects.

The guild meets on a regular basis to do work such as review issues or problems that have come up that require several architects to solve, perform cross-disciplinary work, or plan later working sessions to create or update a broad architectural vision. The guild may also wish to schedule lunch and learn sessions to share knowledge across all architects. The guild may create standards and practices for all architects to follow.

Chapter 5

Design By Contract

Most, if not all, large companies have a workforce spread across many localities or even countries. In addition, most also use some amount of contract labor either through staff augmentation or outsourcing. In addition, many large companies encourage some of their workforce to work from home. In this environment it is extremely important to clearly describe the work that needs to be done by describing the required results, and by making each unit of work as independent as possible.

The benefits this gives you are the ability to give the work to any team anywhere without the overhead of collaboration across distance. You also reduce the time and effort to integrate the work of many teams when releasing the product. You never have to worry about how the work is done as long as the team delivers the required results. This practice removes most issues of time zone differences if each unit of work is given to a team of people who are in the same physical place (which is what I recommend to get the most value from this practice). Note that a team might be just 2 or 3 people.

Design By Contract

Design by contract is a very old engineering technique that has been used almost since there were engineers. Along with standardized measures, it is what gives us the ability to do things such as change just the starter and not replace the whole car when the starter fails. Design by contract was introduced to software at least 40 years before Agile.

The basic technique is to divide something into pieces, then for each piece describe precisely what it needs to start its work (the inputs) and what it provides when it finishes (the outputs). A simple example would be home loans. You can break up the work into origination, underwriting, document preparation, closing, funding, and servicing. Each part is done by a different person. That person can describe exactly what he or she needs to do the job (the inputs) and exactly what he or she will produce at the end (the outputs).

Once the inputs and outputs are identified, it allows each person to do the job with very little need (if any) to interact with the others. Not only that, the other people do not care how the job was done as long as the proper outputs are given. If we wanted to automate this set of processes, we could do just one part at a time, as long as the automation produces the outputs that are required. This is exactly what we want to achieve with design by contract – the ability for each part to be worked on independently of the rest.

Design by contract can be applied to anything. In processes, the contract is often expressed as information. For buildings, a lot of the contract is expressed as building codes and standards. One part of a modular home has connectors in specific places so the modules can be joined together on site. In software, the contract is called an interface. The contract between business and the product delivery teams is typically expressed as requirements which may take the form of mockups, standards, information models, use cases, user stories, conversations, and many other means of expressing information.

Some software practices that implement design by contract include the use of functions, classes, component interfaces, and services. Design by contract is especially powerful when combined with one of the Big Three Management Practices – divide the work into nearly independent pieces. In fact, done properly, dividing the work into work packages is the business equivalent of design by contract. This combination of practices can be found in Object-Oriented Programming (OOP), Component Based Design, and Service Oriented Architecture (SOA).

With design by contract, the contract is described and agreed to before the work to implement that contract is done. Some in the Agile community disagree with doing this because they want to evolve the design as they work. If the whole team is 7 or so people, they have all the skills they need to do the whole job, they are all co-located in time and space, they work only with this team, and the business or end user is constantly available, then the team can evolve the design as they go along. This is actually somewhat less efficient than design by contract, but it is a possible way to work. If any one of those things is not true, then you need design by contract to mitigate the problems that will occur when everyone does not have the same information about what needs to be done. Since the ideal Agile team is quite rare in large companies (due to factors such as assigning people to multiple projects at once, matrix structures, and distributed workforces), doing design by contract reduces risk and saves quite a lot of money over the long term.

What is so Hard About This?

The hard part of design by contract is that a large number of Agile practitioners say it is not necessary. People have to be convinced to do it. If we lived in the perfect Agile world, design by contract becomes less important because the contracts could be evolved over time. But in really large companies, we are unlikely to have the perfect Agile environment, and so design by contract becomes necessary to control risk and prevent integration problems.

Another problem is that a very large percentage of people in product delivery do not know how to do design by contract. As I go from company to company over the years, I am finding fewer and fewer people who know how to produce products using design by contract. Few colleges and universities teach it, and most companies have greatly cut their training budgets over the last 10 years so employees are not getting trained in these techniques. This is a case of being penny wise and dollar foolish. Save pennies today by not training your employees in techniques that keep costs low and lose millions of dollars in increased costs tomorrow. Some individuals will turn to certificate programs and get the training that way, but that is typically a small percentage of your workforce who will pay for the training themselves and take it on their own time.

If you are going for the big win of dividing the work into nearly independent pieces and design by contract together, you have more problems. What I find over and over is that most people in product delivery think they are dividing the work into nearly independent pieces, but an examination of their work shows they are not. I see this with use cases and user stories and I see this with software. I see it less often with hardware because the physicality of the hardware makes it easier for people to see how to divide up the work.

When it comes to software, people following good object-oriented programming practices are doing design by contract. A huge percentage of programmers today are not following object-oriented programming practices. They think they are doing so because they are programming in Java, but that is not necessarily true. People program in Java all the time without using the techniques of object-oriented programming and likewise many people do object-oriented programming in computer languages other than Java. If you are not interviewing or training explicitly for object-oriented programming skills, then many of your Java programmers are not doing object-oriented programming. I know they are not because I have seen their code and it is not object-oriented.

You have a similar issue with component based design and SOA. Your people may be putting their work in multiple files and doing late binding, but that does not mean they are really doing component based design. Your people may be coding web services but that does not mean they are implementing a service oriented architecture.

Because people think they are already doing these practices, it can be very hard to get them to attend training or to change the way they are working. It is a little easier to convince people who are writing software because there are tools such as Sonar that examine the code and tell the programmer where they are not using good practices. If you institute quality measures and standards, the programmers will have to learn better ways of working to meet those standards. The same is true for hardware designs which are typically produced in CAD tools. Those tools will expose problem areas, so if you set standards then the hardware designers will have to learn new practices to meet those standards.

The really difficult area is where the product is described in text and pictures, such as a product that is a training class or a manual, and I want to divide the work of writing it into multiple independent pieces. How do I know the work has been divided into independent pieces before it is written? What you need is someone with a lot of experience in the topic, who is good at dividing work into independent pieces, to look for problems such as lack of independence or clarity. The hard part is finding the expert.

What are the Benefits of the Practice?

If the product work is divided into well-defined pieces, then those pieces can be worked on by anyone at any time. As long as what is produced satisfies the contract, then the parts of the work can be completed independently of each other. This allows you to balance workloads, and by removing the dependencies between teams and individuals, makes it much less likely that one team will be blocked waiting for another team to finish their work. When building a house, the plumbers and electricians each work independently. It does not matter if the electricity is done first, the plumbing is done first, or they are both done together. Each person knows what to do and so does not have to coordinate with the others to get their own work done.

When the time comes to put all the pieces together, to integrate the product, there will be far fewer problems if everyone has done their work according to the contracts. The contracts tell how the pieces fit together so you do not have a last minute effort to redo pieces to make them fit together. Your product should go together just like a puzzle, each piece in its place. This can save significant time (and money) every time the product is released. Imagine, if you could reduce the time to release a product from 6 weeks to 1 week, what that will save you every time there is a release.

Design by contract also saves you money by removing much of the need for different teams, possibly in different parts of the world, to interact. The need for coordination of work across teams, and fixing problems when the coordination fails, has been shown to cost 10% (and often far more) of a project budget. That does not even count the cost of people being delayed waiting for someone else to do their part.

If you combine design by contract with dividing the work into nearly independent pieces, then you get an additional benefit that finding and fixing defects in the product is much easier, which also means cheaper. The hardest to find, most expensive defects are typically in the interactions between multiple parts of the product. A consequence of dividing the product into nearly independent pieces is that each piece encapsulates a set of closely related functionality. When there is a defect in that functionality, there is just one place to look to find that functionality, one place to look to find the defect. Not only is it faster to find the defect, it is also easier to fix since it only has to be fixed in one place. Depending on the nature of the defects, the cost savings can be quite significant. Research suggests that fixing defects can take 50% or more of a project budget, so reducing the cost of fixing defects can lead to significant gains.

Benefit to the Individual
Design by contract helps the individual by making the work she has to complete very well-defined. This way there are fewer questions and fewer mistakes made due to misunderstanding. The implementer is free to do the work any way he wants as long as the contract is met. There are no side effects where someone else's work breaks his code. There is a reduced need to collaborate with other people, which makes distributed teams work better.

82

Benefit to the Project

With design by contract there are fewer integration problems and fewer defects found after integration. Defects are found faster and are typically easier to fix. Because we reduce the need to collaborate, there are fewer miscommunication problems, and fewer meetings. Workload balancing is much easier, and it is easy to add people to the team.

Benefit to the Asset

With design by contract, your product is easier and cheaper to maintain over time. When the implementation work needs to be done, a decision can be made at that time to give the work to employees, contractors, outsource shops, or any combination. Overall this gives you the opportunity for greater business agility.

Benefit to the Portfolio

At the portfolio level you see cost savings and ease of work load balancing across the company.

How to Get Started

Anyone can start this by describing well defined work packages for their work. This includes business work packages such as use cases or user stories, more technical work packages such as component specifications or services, and even management type work packages such as tasks.

The first step would be to create some work packages, such as a list of user stories or a set of tasks. Then for each work package, imagine you will be sending that work package to another company to implement. Describe what the other company can assume to be true about work produced by others and the results you require for each work package they will implement. When the work described in the work package is completed, then what will the product do, what data will be accessible, or what new thing will a person be able to do?

Be very clear on on expectations of quality and performance. If you want a demonstration of progress every week, then make sure that is clear. You also need to state clearly what is to be delivered, such as the product plus all automated test cases that verify its functionality. Or perhaps they must deliver a description of a new process along with the training people will need to follow the new process.

Describing all this does not have to be a lot of work. In many cases, you can reference existing materials by saying something like "the resulting product must conform to the quality standards found here <link to online standards>". Even if the work is being done by different teams within your company, being clear on expectations enables the teams to work independently and yet what they produce fits together.

Chapter 6

Refactoring

Refactor means to restructure. A long-lived product will need to be restructured for a variety of reasons, including making it easier to add new features, accommodating changes in the architecture, and improving the quality measures of the product. When refactoring is standard practice, you increase the valuable lifetime of your product and decrease the total lifetime cost of ownership.

Refactoring

Refactoring is a practice of restructuring a product for the purpose of making it easier to understand and maintain. Refactoring improves the quality of the product without changing the functionality. In general, refactoring simplifies complexity. This is a very old engineering practice that was adopted by software developers from the earliest days of computing. Many of the techniques also apply to data, documents, processes, and hardware.

When a product is small it is easy to keep it well-structured. As it grows in size, it is easy to introduce inconsistencies, duplication, and poor structure. Often the product needs to be refactored to add new features that were not anticipated when the product was first designed.

When an implementer is in the habit of refactoring, it becomes a normal part of his everyday work. He notices something not quite right in the structure of the product and fixes it. Working this way maintains the structure of the product at the same time that new features are being added. Refactoring should be an integral part of product delivery.

Extreme Programming practitioners say code first, then refactor. In my own work, I often found the opposite to work as well. I refactored first to make it easier to add new features that were not anticipated when the code was first structured. When writing books and documents I use both approaches; sometimes I write then refactor, sometimes I refactor before writing the next bit because as I plan the next bit I see how restructuring will make the upcoming work easier.

What is so Hard About This?

People call refactoring "rework" and say that it is bad. I must disagree. Often the product was structured very well for what it did initially. Typically as the years go by, the users ask for things we never anticipated. We restructure the product to easily accommodate the new features. It is just part of what you do to maintain the product over the long term to increase its usable life. This is similar to putting a solid state drive into an old computer to increase its usable life. How could this be considered bad? If we do not restructure, we may create a mess. That is bad.

There is a perception that refactoring takes a lot of time. There is a fear that if the implementation team does refactoring they will not meet project deadlines and will be late getting features to market. It is true that time spent refactoring is time not spent developing a new feature. But the point of the refactoring is to make subsequent work faster and easier.

Of course there is a learning curve. Many people have not thought about refactoring and do not know how to do it. While learning refactoring techniques, the work will go slower. This should be planned for, with extra time allowed in the schedule for learning to refactor. Notice I said the extra time is for learning. The actual time spent refactoring will be made up by making the product easier to maintain.

The hard sell for refactoring is when the product work is structured as projects. It may happen that this particular project team has the cost of refactoring and a later project team gets the benefit. Project managers do not like the idea that their project will pay for someone else to be more efficient. The implementers are generally not rewarded for refactoring and there may be negative consequences if the work to make the product easier to maintain means some anticipated features are not developed or the project is late.

This should not be true for people skilled at refactoring unless the product is so poorly structured that the refactoring is a large effort (and especially when there are no tests for the existing product). Anything refactored has to be tested, so if the tests do not exist they have to be written and run on the existing product, then run again after each refactoring to ensure nothing is broken. In a large refactoring effort, writing the tests can take a lot of time.

A very effective way to teach people to refactor is to embed some people who know how to refactor into the team as player/coaches. Each player/coach sits side by side with another person and they work together on the product, with the coach showing how to refactor as the opportunities arise. Instead of sitting in a classroom learning techniques they may never use, the product delivery team directly applies the appropriate techniques (identified by the coach) as they are developing the product.

I am often asked if a refactoring project should be created just to do some refactoring work on existing products. There is a lot of resistance to this idea because it is seen as pure overhead and the benefit is in the future. Most of the time it is not necessary to do this. Products can be refactored over time as the different teams work on normal updates and fixes to the products. In addition, if refactoring becomes just part of everyone's job, then everyone learns it (not just the refactoring team).

Refactoring is almost certainly going on already without anyone talking about it. In my early career, I was a top ranked programmer. I never talked with my bosses about refactoring. It never occurred to me to do so because it was just part of my job. Though I produce many different kinds of products today, I still make it a practice to refactor as I work. It is part of what enables me to work so much faster.

Proposing a refactoring initiative may generate a lot of resistance. It is easier to find some top notch implementers who already do refactoring, then put them into teams with the directive to not just implement product but also to mentor others in refactoring.

What are the Benefits of the Practice?

Poorly structured products are hard to understand. This makes them time consuming to update and makes it more likely that defects will be introduced when changes are made to the product. I once was asked to make a simple update to some code. It was so hard to understand that it took me a week to figure out how it worked. I spent a half day making changes so the code made sense and then put in the update. When I came back to that code base several months later, I could understand it in a few minutes, and so the updates went much faster. Many people have told me of similar experiences in their careers.

Refactoring generally takes a small amount of time to do but makes subsequent work on the product much faster. This is a practice where spending a little time now saves a lot of time later. Refactoring also makes it less likely that defects will be introduced due to lack of understanding how the code works.

For some products, refactoring as the product is updated will save money by preventing future problems. For other products, refactoring will greatly reduce the amount of time it takes to maintain the product today. How much money refactoring will save your company is impossible to quantify, but some examples can help you understand the value of the practice.

Many large long-lived companies still have mainframe computers with software written in COBOL. Some of those systems are 30-40 years old. In some cases the companies have not replaced those systems because they work so well. The system rarely has a problem and is easy to maintain so there is no value in replacing it. By refactoring the software to keep it understandable throughout the years, the software has provided value to the company for many decades.

I know of other companies with systems only 10 years old that are already a mess. No one is allowed to make changes to the system because it always creates a problem when they do. The software is so poorly structured that no one can figure out how to work with it. I know of a number of instances like this where the company put together new software and databases as a front end to the existing system, then added new features in the new software and kept calling the old software for the old features.

In one case, this was a commercial product that included hardware. The new software did not work on the old hardware and the old software could not be ported to the new hardware because no one understood it. The company ended up installing two computers at their customer sites instead of one.

In other cases I know of, the company decided it was better to replace the old system because it was so hard to maintain. They surveyed employees to find out who used the system and for what. Then they bought software to replace the old system, turned off the old system, found out what broke, and made the fixes at great expense to the company.

Software, databases, or documentation do not have to "go bad" and be replaced periodically. With care, they can have a very long lifetime, and you can avoid the expensive, risky projects to replace them.

Benefit to the Individual
Once in the habit of refactoring, the work of enhancing and maintaining the product is faster and easier.

Benefit to the Project
When the product is refactored so it is easy to maintain and enhance, fewer defects are introduced, and those defects are easier to find and fix. Eventually, more work gets done in the same amount of time.

Benefit to the Asset
Refactoring gives your product a longer useful lifetime. It also

reduces the lifetime cost of ownership. Any updates to your product are faster and less expensive. Making the product easier to change gives you the opportunity for greater business agility.

Benefit to the Portfolio

At the portfolio level you see higher quality and cost savings across the company.

How to Get Started

The main thing to do is not let the managers prevent refactoring as a misguided way to reduce cost. This will be difficult if you only reward the managers for delivering their project on time and budget and do not reward them for considering the long term benefit to the company. That change to metrics can have a widespread impact and so may be difficult to do. Another possibility is to create budgets and schedules that are a little larger than you think they need to be so that the implementers have the time to learn and adopt practices such as refactoring (and do not let the sponsor use the extra budget to add new features).

In addition, when setting performance goals for your implementers include asking them to learn and make use of the software engineering practices and be sure the managers are aware that the implementers are being required to do this. When the product is software, there are quality tools such as Sonar that can be used before and after refactoring to show that the refactoring improved the quality of the code (which is one way to know if refactoring is being done).

But be careful to avoid a brute force approach where everyone is required to refactor all the time. When working on legacy code, it may be impractical to refactor it because the cost is much too high compared to the benefit. Give the implementers the time in the schedule to apply refactoring, and trust the senior people to tell you when it is not practical to do so.

Chapter 7

Quality Practices

We live in a world where sloppiness has replaced quality and dilettantes have replaced professionals. Get it done quick and cheap seems to be all that is important. And yet, we all personally appreciate quality products and services when we encounter them. If brash, young internet companies such as Facebook and Google are finding that quality really does matter for their businesses, then today's long-established companies are well-advised to look to the quality of their own products if they want to be viable and relevant in the years to come.

The benefits of quality practices for software are that anyone can understand and maintain the code (so you don't get "one deep" in knowledge), fewer bugs are introduced into the code as it is enhanced, the code has a longer useful lifetime, and the total cost of ownership is lower. Contrast that with the short term gain of bringing in a project cheaper today by getting rid of the quality practices and incurring far greater expense in the future.

Quality Practices

Quality practices are important for every product. In this section I discuss quality practices for software. Software is such a big part of everything we do that improving the quality of the software goes a long way toward improving all our products.

In the past, programmers were trained in some basic coding and testing quality practices that were considered an integral part of the job of programming. A programmer made sure her code was of high quality before giving it to the test team. The job of the test team was to integrate the work of many programmers and test across a large body of code. Gradually over the last 20 years it has changed where programmers no longer verify the quality of their own code, but expect testers to do that work as well. However quality is about more than testing, and some of the practices to achieve quality have to be done by the programmers while they are coding.

Over at least the last 20 years, there has been a market driven push to get more software out faster, and at the same time to spend less money. Each project's schedule and budget is ever smaller compared to the amount of work to be delivered. In this situation, the first thing to get dropped is quality. I know companies who have not measured code quality for more than a decade because they know that quality practices are not being followed. The result of this is code that is increasingly hard to work with, which means it takes longer and longer to make updates or add features. We are paying today for poorly thought out cost and time saving measures of the past.

Many people are turning to Agile in an attempt to be better, faster, and cheaper. But when you have a large amount of poor quality code, adopting Agile is not going to help. There are practices such as refactoring that will gradually make the code easier and faster to maintain. At the same time, you need to re-institute the quality practices of the past to keep from getting back into the same situation.

One of the most fundamental quality practices is to embed error checking and error handling into the code itself. Comments about why the code is written the way it is should be a standard part of every software unit. Most functions should have a small amount of code. Standard formatting rules should be followed to make the code easy to read. The code should be structured so that each unit is strongly cohesive, loosely coupled, and mostly independent. There should not be duplication of code (the same code in multiple places). The programmer should test his code to verify it works, and those tests should be automated and included in a regression test suite. Shame on any programmer whose code can be made to crash by the test team!

There are software tools such as Sonar that examine code looking for a variety of quality measures such as code duplication and complexity. The tools can be configured with just the things you want to look for. You can set them up initially to look for a few critical quality measures and let your teams get up to speed on those practices. Then later add a couple more quality measures. Over time the programmers will have learned better programming practices and the code will be easier to maintain.

What is so Hard About This?

The programmers don't want to do it. They just want to hack code, not work in a disciplined way. Many programmers think Agile means no discipline – they are wrong. Agile is most likely more disciplined than how the individual programmers work today.

When you divide the work up into development versus maintenance, there is no benefit to a development programmer to do the job well, because maintaining the code is someone else's problem. Even though Google does not have separate development and maintenance teams, they still had a problem because developing code was separate from testing the quality of the code. The developers were not rewarded for producing high quality code.

The book, "How Google Tests Software" by James A. Whittaker, Jason Arbon, and Jeff Carollo describes the steps Google had to take to put quality practices into place, and how hard it was to get programmers doing quality practices. They are a young company but already had a mess and took big steps to fix it.

People will say that it takes longer to program something if they have to follow the quality practices. It is true that it takes a little more time when the code is being developed. But most of your programmers are spending most of their time updating and fixing existing software, not creating something completely new. In the short term all programming work will take longer as the programmers insert quality factors into existing code. Once the quality factors are in place, updates to existing code should go much faster.

Management may be contributing to the problem by insisting the work be done faster than the programmers say they can do it. If an experienced team says it will take them 3 weeks to do something, and management insists they do it in 2 weeks, something will be left out to make that deadline. Most commonly it is quality practices and testing.

I know several very large companies whose software projects always complete on time and budget. Often the code that is delivered does not completely work and has a lot of defects. So they start another project to fix that code, and the second project also completes on time and budget. You get what you measure, and they measure time and budget. They can honestly claim 100% success on those factors.

Their customers do not care about the projects, they care about what is delivered to them. If it is a mess when they get it and they have to wait for another project to be done to fix it, you may lose them as customers. In today's markets, where your customers have a lot of choices, you can't afford to lose customers over quality issues. Someone else will get it right.

What are the Benefits of the Practice?

Benefit to the Individual

About 10% of programming work in the world is creating new software. About 90% of the programming work in the world is enhancing or fixing existing software. It makes more sense to make maintaining the software faster since that is where most of your budget is spent and if that software has fewer defects, we can spend more of that 90% on new features and less on fixing problems. Spend a little more on creating the software so it is of good quality to save a lot over the lifetime of the software.

Facebook thinks this is so important that they put their most brilliant software engineers to work in their quality group which is chartered to create tools and find other ways to help Facebook programmers create better quality software. Google did the same. These are today multibillion dollar companies who think that a quality product is so important they pay a lot of money to hire the best engineers to focus on quality. For the users, fewer features that work every time is better than a lot of features of poor quality.

It is pretty likely that your company does not sell software, so you may think this is not so important. But your company probably depends very heavily on software. Higher quality software can be enhanced and maintained more efficiently, so that saves you money. Higher quality software also works better from the users' perspective, so it enhances their ability to be effective at running the company. Updates to higher quality software are faster, so the users do not have to wait a long time to get a fix or an important feature.

Benefit to the Project
In the short term, implementers will complain about having to do these quality practices. The first time one of them gets to enhance high quality code, he will see how much easier it is than working on poor quality code.

Benefit to the Asset
Keeping quality high for the product means it has a longer usable lifetime and a lower lifetime cost of ownership. This means you have more money for new features. Those features will also be faster to implement, providing the opportunity for greater business agility.

Benefit to the Portfolio
High quality throughout the company leads to the lowest overall operating costs.

How to Get Started

The main thing to do is to add quality metrics as a project metric so the managers have an incentive to encourage high quality products. Without the quality metric, managers will optimize on what they are rewarded for, time and budget, and if money is running out, quality will suffer because they are not being paid to deliver quality. That change to metrics can have a widespread impact and so it may be difficult to do.

Another possibility is to create budgets and schedules that are a little larger than you think they need to be so that the implementers have the time to learn and adopt the quality practices. But you have to be sure quality is what the money is being spent on and not being used to add more features.

In addition, when setting performance goals for your implementers include asking them to learn and make use of the quality practices and be sure the managers are aware that the implementers are being required to do this. But be careful to avoid a brute force approach where you ask the implementers to add these quality factors into code they are not otherwise enhancing. When working on legacy code, it may be impractical to add in some of the quality measures, such as looking for strong cohesion, loose coupling, and lack of duplication, because the cost is much too high compared to the benefit. Give the implementers the time in the schedule to apply the quality practices, and trust the senior people to tell you when it is not practical to do so.

Chapter 8

Frameworks, Stubs, and Mock Objects

Frameworks, stubs, and mock objects are used in software development primarily to allow earlier testing or to simplify testing. They may also be used to outline a solution that is fully implemented later, much as an author creates a table of contents and outlines each chapter before writing the detailed contents of the book.

Because frameworks, stubs, and mock objects let us start testing sooner, we can discover and correct problems much earlier when it is least expensive. With the complexity of software today, there is often no feasible way to test some parts of the product without a framework, stub, or mock object.

Frameworks, Stubs, and Mock Objects

Frameworks are used in software development to enable some kinds of otherwise manual testing to be automated. This is reduces the cost of testing. When a test is run manually you have the cost of a person's time each time the test is run. When the test is automated, you have the cost of a person's time to write the test, and almost no cost after that. Since we almost never run a test just once, automated testing saves a lot of money over the long term.

Frameworks are things that allow you to automate testing by making it seem that a person has done something to interact with your product. The framework mimics user actions such as entering data or clicking a link. Frameworks may mimic hardware that is not yet completed. General purpose frameworks can be purchased for things such as load testing or performance testing a product. Other times, frameworks may be developed by your implementers to support the long-term maintenance of a product.

Stubs are used in software development to enable earlier integration and end-to-end testing than might otherwise be possible. The earlier the team can test the integrated solution, the faster they find problems, and most of the time the problems are much less expensive to fix than if they were found at the end of the project.

Stubs are pieces of code that represent a part of your product that has not yet been implemented. They behave in a limited way like that part of the product. Because they are limited, they are very fast to create. Over time more code is added to the stub until it is no longer a stub, it is the complete code.

Mock objects are the same kind of idea as a stub, but where most people think of stubs at a function level, mock objects are complete objects that behave in a limited way like a part of the product that is not yet implemented. They have the same benefits as stubs. Sometimes we use stubs and mock objects in testing even if that part of the product is already implemented because it reduces the amount of code that has to be reviewed when a defect is found. The less code to be reviewed, the faster it is to find defects, which reduces the cost of fixing defects.

What is so Hard About This?

Stubs and mock objects are by nature incomplete and have to be redone later to make them complete. Managers get worried when people are working on something that they plan to revisit. There is a concern that we are doing unnecessary work and therefore generating unnecessary cost. That concern is why we make stubs and mock objects as small as possible and create them as quickly as possible to keep the cost low. That cost is made up later in the project by finding and fixing defects earlier and faster.

Programmers are told to avoid rework as though it is inherently bad. But rework is actually what we need to do to maintain high quality products. The products we create are, for the most part, so large and complex it is not possible we will get everything right the first time. We will have to test and learn and redo. Planning to rework a stub or mock object into the full solution is a small price to pay to enable earlier testing of the code when it is cheaper and faster to fix.

You do want to avoid unnecessary rework. This is rework that is the result of poor programming practices or lack of planning. You also have ensure there is a balance of cost and benefit. Sometimes people go overboard, doing more work than they need to do on things that will be replaced. Or they spend too much time setting up the frameworks to do things that are not important for that particular project. People experienced with these practices should work with a team that wants to adopt them to guide the team to doing the right amount of work with frameworks, stubs, and mock objects.

What are the Benefits of the Practice?

The use of frameworks, stubs, and mock objects lets us automate testing of more parts of the product than we could before. This allows us to do more testing and faster testing which allows us to find and fix defects faster. Frameworks are especially helpful when testing for load on a system. We can simulate a load of huge numbers of users and look for problems before the product is released to market.

This approach should have been used with the healthcare.gov website which had major issues with capacity from the very beginning. Testing for capacity, the load on the system, would have exposed those problems so that they could have been fixed before the site went public.

Using stubs and mock objects lets us integrate and find integration problems earlier. We can find defects in the interactions between parts earlier and fix them faster. This also lets us test the architecture, the structure, of the product before the functionality is in place. The relatively small cost of creating stubs and mock objects is made up with higher quality code sooner.

This is another approach that should have been used on the healthcare.gov website. There were multiple contractors working on the site and they put off end-to-end testing until the end when they ran out of time to do it. Using stubs and mock objects to integrate incomplete work would have allowed for earlier end-to-end testing so there would have been time to find and fix the problems.

I have used stubs in the past as a way to indicate where the actual code would plug into the system once it was complete. This is a big advantage when you don't know all the requirements up front, but you do know where that functionality is going to be implemented. I know many people who use stubs to create plugin points for future functionality. On one very large, very long project I was involved with, many people came to the project and left well before it was finished. The stubs were a convenient way to show where the various bits of functionality needed to be implemented and helped new people get up to speed faster.

Benefit to the Individual

The big win to using frameworks, stubs, and mock objects is that the implementer is able to test more things and earlier than without them. This enables the implementer to find defects faster and fix them earlier when it is least expensive.

Benefit to the Project

Frameworks, stubs, and mock objects let the test team start sooner, overlapping their work with the implementation work. This helps the project complete on schedule while maintaining high quality. The net result is that there are seldom late serious defects in the project, nor do you have to delay releasing the product because there has not been enough time to test it.

Benefit to the Asset

Since stubs and mock objects will be replaced before the product is delivered, the long term benefit to the product is the frameworks. The frameworks will still exist after a project is over and that allows you to use them to test the code in later projects when enhancements are made to the product. In addition, the product is of higher quality and therefore will have a longer usable life and lower overall cost of ownership.

Benefit to the Portfolio

The use of frameworks, stubs, and mock objects supports higher quality products which have a longer usable life and lower overall cost of ownership. Costs of maintaining and enhancing the products is lower so more money is available for developing new things.

How to Get Started

Frameworks, stubs, and mock objects are not always needed. A team wishing to use them should analyze the work to see if these tools will help the team test the product earlier or make some kinds of testing possible. The team might be interested in using stubs and mock objects to create an outline for the current work that will be filled in as the project progresses. This can make it easier to add implementers to the team later. Be sure the managers are educated in why and when it is important to use frameworks, stubs, and mock objects so the managers do not prevent the use of them when it makes sense to do so.

It is good to bring people skilled in using frameworks, stubs, and mock objects to mentor a team wishing to use these techniques. It is much easier for people to learn these skills as they are needed than to sit in a class being shown examples that may not apply to their actual work.

Section Three

The eXtreme Programming (XP) Practices

Balance is good, because one extreme or the other leads to misery.

- Trent Reznor

An Introduction to the Practices

Extreme Programming is a group of practices for software development. It is called Extreme because it took many existing software development practices to the extreme. Extreme Programming requires the whole team to be in a room together working. Every single person who is part of the implementation effort has to be together, including the customer. Most of the XP practices depend on co-location and dedication in order to be effective. If your teams are distributed, especially when people are working on multiple projects at the same time, then trying to do the XP practices anyway will actually make matters worse than they are today.

Any project teams that are not dedicated and co-located should use practices other than XP to be more efficient and effective. The Big Five Engineering Practices were designed to organize the work of large, distributed, non-dedicated workforces. It is often possible within a large project or program to create some small, dedicated, co-located teams and those individual teams may be able to make use of the XP practices even if the project as a whole cannot. Then you get more efficiency overall from the Big Five Engineering Practices and some teams will get an additional boost from the XP practices.

It is generally better to use XP on smaller efforts than on large efforts. This is because in many ways, XP represents a brute force approach to software development. As one example, instead of thinking about what needs to be tested, the developers are encouraged to write a test case for every line of code. But this causes its own problems as the code base and test suite grow ever larger. Eventually testing takes so long you are unable to do the frequent testing which gives you more benefit than testing every line of code. Then you have to find skilled testing professionals to fix that problem (as both Google and Facebook have discovered).

Because XP requires co-location and dedication of the team to be effective, it tends to be a poor fit for very large corporations. Changing corporate structures to make every team dedicated and co-located is a much bigger change than most large companies want to make. For this reason, most companies implement just a few of the practices and not the full set, or they create a few dedicated and co-located teams in areas such as Innovation where they want the teams to be able to work fast and pivot quickly.

In the next two chapters, I have divided the list of XP practices into those that in my experience do not work very well in large corporate environments and those that are more possible. For those that are more possible, I identify some adjustments that may need to be made to the practices for them to be implemented.

Chapter 9

XP Practices That May Be Infeasible

T he set of practices in this chapter were introduced by the developers of XP. These are the practices that are extreme versions of older software engineering practices, introduced because of problems with poor implementation of the older practices. While not wrong to do, these practices are intended for small, co-located, dedicated teams that do not need to share information outside the team. In practice they do not scale well in large corporations nor to large code bases.

Some of the issues with these practices are that the team loses the ability to easily communicate what they are doing outside of the team, distribute work, work from home, and interact with more than one user. These practices are:

1. Whole Team
2. Automated Customer Tests
3. Simple Design
4. Design Improvement
5. Metaphor
6. Test First Development

Whole Team

Whole Team (which requires EVERYONE involved in the initiative to be physically co-located, including the customer or project sponsor) is infeasible in most large companies. In large companies it is highly unlikely the project sponsor (the Customer) will sit full time with the team telling them what to do and answering questions. Another problem with Whole Team is that in large companies the customer is seldom the user. The people who can tell what the solution needs to be are the users, not the customer. And since there are typically a lot of users, what is needed is a user advocate to represent the whole community of users. The user advocate works with the implementation team, not the customer.

To illustrate the difference between customer and user, I'll relate a true story from a major defense contractor in the USA. At one time, this company decided to replace their accounting system with something more modern. Salespeople from many vendors came and demonstrated their solutions to accounting managers and their bosses who were the customers. A solution was chosen, and a long project was implemented to install and customize it.

The day for deployment arrived, which was the first time the accountants (the users) saw the system. The accountants pointed out that the system was impossible for them to use. The managers, who were not accountants, had chosen a commercial accounting system. The defense contractor was required by law to do government style accounting which is very different. They had to throw out the system and start over. You do not want the customer specifying the requirements of the system, you want the users specifying the requirements of the system.

Whole Team as described in XP makes it difficult and expensive to have work from home or to distribute the work in any way, including the use of vendors or outsourcing. While Whole Team may be possible in some places in a large company, it will not be possible across the entire company. So a different approach should be taken that supports teams who are co-located and those who are not. One such approach is to describe well defined work packages that are distributed to teams in accordance with agreed upon contracts.

Automated Customer Tests

The practice of Automated Customer Tests is not very feasible in large companies because the Customer is typically the Project Sponsor and not the user. Therefore the Customer probably has no idea how to test the product, much less what kinds of tests can be automated. In addition, I don't know of anyone in a role of Project Sponsor who is likely to want to write these tests.

This practice should be replaced with tests described by user advocates and testers, with the User Acceptance Testing performed by actual end users. We should not require these tests to be automated. Automated Customer Tests do make sense for verifying basic functionality. But ultimately what we want is actual users interacting with the software and providing feedback on what they want to do with the software and how they expect it to work.

When possible, getting some of the actual users to do frequent User Acceptance Testing (not just once at the end) is a very powerful technique that leads to the best feedback so that problems are found much earlier and there is high acceptance by the users once the product is delivered. I have used this approach often and with great success. It is far superior to asking a customer to describe tests that are run automatically.

One team I know who got the customer to write the tests discovered the hard way that the customer is not the user, and automation is no substitute for a person interacting with your product. The team had developed a mobile app that allowed a person to use voice prompts to do a variety of actions with their bank account, such as getting a balance. The team had worked with the project sponsor to write tests and these tests were automated. The sponsor frequently reviewed their work and was pleased. Test coverage was high.

Then the team put an early version of the app in front of real users and found all kinds of serious problems with how the app worked. The sponsor had made a number of assumptions that were not true. Fixing the problems required significant redesign of the app. Though the app worked exactly as the sponsor said it should, real users interacted differently with the app than was assumed. The product turned out to be unusable in real life. You want real users doing User Acceptance Test.

Evolving Design

Simple Continuous Design and Design Improvement are practices that allow a design to evolve over time. They are really good ideas when implemented within a well-thought-out architecture. But in XP these practices replace doing architecture and high level design with continual evolution of the design.

While evolving the design is possible with small co-located teams, allowing everyone to evolve the architecture and overall design as they go along does not work with large distributed teams. In this situation, which is common in large companies, up-front design and architecture (which XP does not even address) are important mechanisms for structuring the work of a large distributed team.

This is not to say that the design should be locked in stone. The design should be considered fluid and changeable, but these changes need to be made in a controlled manner to avoid chaos throughout and integration problems every time you want to make a release. Design of the small, for example within an independent component or function, can be safely left to individuals or small co-located teams to change as needed. When the design change impacts other teams, then there has to be coordination. A well-defined architecture provides the means for that coordination.

When working with distributed teams, especially large teams, describing an overall architecture provides a way for people who are not together all the time to understand how each person's or small team's work fits into the overall effort. This solves a couple of potential problems. It makes it much more likely that the code will fit together when it is integrated, it prevents having multiple people unknowingly repeat work that was already done, and it allows individual implementers the freedom to make the best choices for their work without negatively impacting the rest of the team.

Architecture is also an important way to communicate to people outside the team what the team is working on. Since very little work in a large company is truly completely independent, it is likely that people outside the project team will need to know what is being worked on. In addition, a documented architecture provides valuable information for future projects that modify this same code.

In long projects, a documented architecture is invaluable for getting new team members up to speed on the work that needs to be done. This is because an architecture describes how the code is put together. Without the architecture, a new team member would have to look at large amounts of code to determine what it does and where their work fits in. In large teams, especially when distributed, describing and documenting the overall architecture of a system is a better practice than letting the team members evolve it in the code over time.

Metaphor

Metaphor is an expression of how the program works. Metaphor is possibly meant to replace the practice of using architectural and design patterns with a description the team makes up for themselves.

The problem with letting the team make up their own description rather than using a well-defined one is that the metaphor is likely to not make sense outside the team. Patterns are described and published to enhance communication. Using patterns enables team members to communicate with people outside the team, possibly in the form of papers, blog posts, articles, presentations at conferences, or even people who work on the code in a later project. A metaphor understood by only the team blocks communication outside the team. This also means it is harder to get a new person up-to-speed. Metaphor should be replaced with a return to patterns.

Metaphor in XP is also expressed as naming conventions. This is good practice, but even better is that the naming conventions use the language of the domain in which we are working. If the team makes up their own naming conventions, again this may not make sense to anyone outside the team. Using the language of the domain has been a recommended practice since COBOL (a computer language specifically designed so that programs could be written in the language of business).

The danger of metaphor is that it can inhibit communication outside of the current team. Instead of metaphors invented by each team, it is better to use defined architectural and design patterns to describe how the code works because these are understood by most implementers. In addition, naming conventions should use the language of the domain, such as banking, insurance, games, or personal productivity, and not be something made up by the team that only they understand.

Test First Development

XP's version of test-driven development is typically called test first development because in XP developers write the tests before they write the code that will be tested. The developer puts the tests into a system that runs them automatically without needing manual intervention.

I am a huge fan of developers doing their own testing. Every good programmer I know does it. About a decade ago, as jobs became even more specialized, someone decided programmers do not test, only testers test. There are a lot of very basic tests that the developer can do as part of the process of writing code. The developer quickly finds and fixes low-level problems without needing to get anyone else involved. Asking a tester to do that work is very inefficient and wasteful. Test-driven development as described in XP puts the responsibility for basic testing back on the programmer, which is good. The focus on automated testing is also excellent because automated testing is much faster and less expensive than manual testing.

On the other hand, there is no real need to write the test first if you do a little design before starting to code. I know many highly rated programmers who have never written a test before writing the code, though they do plan how to test before writing the code. They produce extremely high quality code.

As a counter argument, one friend of mine who is a fan of writing tests first likes it because he says it forces some thought about design. He also believes most programmers are not able to design before coding. He thinks test first development is a good substitute for a lack of design skills.

A more serious problem with test first development is something that XP proponents think is good. They like test first development because it produces nearly 100% test coverage almost effortlessly. (100% test coverage means every line of code is associated with a test).

100% test coverage in almost all cases is not necessary and it causes problems over time. As the code base gets larger so does the set of tests. The number of tests becomes so large that it is impossible to integrate the code frequently (a very important practice to keep projects on time and budget) because of how long it takes to run all the tests every time. In some cases the test code is larger than than the code for the product itself.

In the past, 100% test coverage was never considered except for safety critical applications and some finance applications (where the cost of failure is so high it is worth the expense of 100% test coverage). Even in those systems, typically only some critical parts have 100% test coverage.

In general, the overall cost of 100% test coverage far outweighs the benefits. I know hardware is cheap and processors are fast. But even the largest, fastest systems can be quickly overwhelmed by huge test suites developed because we want 100% test coverage. There is a lot of extremely high quality code in the world that does not have 100% test coverage. It has the right amount of test coverage.

Test first development is a brute force approach to testing which replaces the careful consideration of what and how to test that has been the hallmark of quality software for decades. Programmer testing should not mean we require a test for every line of code, nor should it mean we require the programmer to write the test before the code. Instead, we should reinstitute test planning and test the right amount of code.

Whether the programmer writes the test before or after writing the code is not important. What is important is that the right tests are written and run.

Chapter 10

XP Practices Feasible for Large Companies

These practices were recommended long before there was Extreme Programming. They were already practiced by good implementers. The demise of many good software engineering practices mostly came because of a push to deliver faster and faster. XP did us a favor by refocusing on what is important. The XP practices we should maintain are:

1. Planning Game
2. Small Releases
3. Continuous Integration
4. Collective Code Ownership
5. Coding Standards
6. Sustainable Pace
7. Pair Programming

Planning Game

Planning releases and increments is important. It is even more important to let the plans adjust based on lessons learned. So many companies point proudly to the fact that all of their projects finish on time and on budget. What they do not tell you is that the resulting product is unusable so they have to schedule a follow on project to fix it (which also completes on time and on budget).

It is very likely today that estimates are padded by the implementation team because they know the time and budget will be cut. They try to pad the estimate enough that when the budget is cut, they can still complete on time.

These are time-wasting games to be playing. Let the team honestly estimate the work, and then believe them and do not cut the budget. If they did over-estimate, then you have money left over to use somewhere else. If the estimate is correct, you will need that time to deliver a quality product the first time, and you will not have to schedule follow-up work to fix it.

One of the things that XP helped us focus on was having the people who will do the work be the same people who estimate the work. The Planning Game as described in XP depends on people all being together, but adjustments can be made so that the appropriate input is received from each team member when releases and increments are planned.

Small Releases

Small releases are a great advantage for every effort, not just Agile. I have used this practice to great benefit on Waterfall projects. The primary benefit to this practice is that we find problems earlier when it is much less expensive to fix them. This has been recommended practice for a very long time and so it is part of the Big Three Management Practices (incremental delivery of solution). You can find a lot of details on this practice in section 1.

Small here is relative. XP teams want to release every week or two, but that may be infeasible for a number of reasons. The code base may be too large for any significant work to be completed in 1-2 weeks. Releasing that often may overwhelm the users. You may have a need or desire to capitalize the work and 1-2 weeks of work is insufficient to be able to do that.

Releases should be short enough that the implementation team gets frequent and early feedback from end users. Releases should be long enough to provide value to the users. It may be that some of the releases go to only a small subset of users for feedback, and several of these releases are collected together to release at once to the whole user population. This can get the frequent feedback desired by the implementers without creating the problems of overwhelming the users or being forced to expense everything.

Continuous Integration

Continuous Integration is not actually continuous, but as a practice it encourages very frequent integration and testing of the code base, sometimes several times a day. This allows the team to find problems that occur in the interactions between their individual components. Good teams have always integrated as often as they could given the limitations of memory and processing power, the size of the code base, and the size of the test suite.

Automation of testing, which you need to make this work, has been available for far longer than XP has been around, though it is much easier to do today than in the past. A well-defined architecture and design by contract are important practices to make integration of code as short and easy a process as possible so that it can be done frequently.

There should not be a goal to integrate and test the code several times a day. Rather the goal should be to integrate and test as frequently as possible to provide value in the form of early feedback to the team.

In general we aim to integrate code at least daily when that is possible. This is because in one day there is not much new code produced, so when new defects are found, there is not much code to review to find and fix the problems. In addition, if a bad approach is discovered, or a requirement was misunderstood, not much time was put into the wrong way of doing things before the mistake was found. This makes it faster to deliver high quality code.

In the past, slow processors and small memories made it impossible to integrate and test code frequently. Daily integrations were possible when the code base was tiny, but as products matured it took longer and longer to integrate the code. I know of one program in the past where it took a week to integrate the code, and then the testing could start. When problems were found, they were big problems that took a lot of time to resolve.

Today, we can take advantage of much faster processors and much larger memory, and so a goal of at least daily integration is possible for many teams. Even still, I know companies with large code bases where on a fast machine with a lot of memory it still takes 8-12 hours (essentially overnight) to integrate and test the code. Google reached this point, but they had seen a lot of value in daily integrations. To be able to continue integrating daily, they had to restructure their test suites and their approach to integration and testing to make it possible.

Collective Code Ownership

Collective Code Ownership means that anyone can, and is allowed to, work on any part of the code. This is different from assigning an owner to a component of the code and requiring all changes to go through that owner.

Typically teams have used the approach of assigning an owner to a section of code because that owner is an expert in that code. They are concerned that anyone else will "mess up" the code and cause it to fail. The problem is that the owner becomes a blockage, a hindrance to getting work done. Someone has to ask the owner for a change and wait until the change is made. They may be blocked from getting some work done while waiting for that change. What if the change is needed when the owner of the code is on vacation?

Ownership of code also has the issue that if only one person knows how it works, you put your company at risk of no one knowing that code or being able to change it if that person leaves. You are "one deep" in knowledge. Some companies solve this by having two owners, but that is still not enough people to really remove the risks. Instead of trying to determine how many owners you need for the code, let everyone know how all the code works, so anyone can work on anything.

The best way to get to this point is to have the experts on the code do pair programming (described below) with other people as they make changes to that part of the code. As the pairs rotate around, over time everyone understands all the code. Any change needed can be made by anyone available without the risk of making a mistake through lack of understanding.

Of course there may be some things that truly do require deep expert knowledge to change, such as scientific algorithms or specific legal language to put on a website. But those areas can be well-documented with information on which experts to consult before making a change.

Collective code ownership is much easier when the team uses the same coding standards and maintains a suite of automated tests that are run each time a change is made. Pair programming makes it much easier to get everyone up to speed on all the code.

Collective ownership may be difficult to do for many reasons. Reporting hierarchies may limit people to work on only certain code. The code may be so poorly structured that leaning how it works takes too much time to get everyone knowledgeable enough to work on it. Performance reviews may be set up in such a way that learning a new system is not rewarded. Finally, security may be concerned that having everyone know all the code is a risk if you happen to have an angry employee trying to cause problems for the company. You have to decide if the business continuity benefit of having many people understand the code is worth the cost of change.

Coding Standards

Coding standards include things such as how to format the code for readability, how to name different kinds of elements within a program, and even the maximum size of a function. Coding standards make all the code look like it was written by one person. This makes it possible for anyone on the team to be able to easily look at any code written by anyone on the team and makes collective ownership feasible. Otherwise, each person spends too much time understanding code written by someone else.

When I was first a programmer out of college, we had strict coding standards to adhere to. There was also a process to get a waiver. I remember I once had to make my case to get a waiver from the coding standard. I had to show the consequence of following the standard and why breaking it was actually better in that one particular instance. I really appreciated the standards when I had to work on code someone else had written.

Many programmers will complain about following a standard, but it really becomes habit over time. Then they don't even think about it anymore. They just do it. Over time a lot of money is saved, and mistakes due to misunderstandings are removed. This is because when everyone follows the same coding standards, the code is much easier to read, therefore it is much faster to understand what needs to be programmed next and how to do it.

Sustainable Pace

Waterfall projects have a rhythm that is typically something like this; the project starts and everyone knows what the first milestone is. The team may not work very hard at first, because very likely they just had a big push to finish the previous project and they are tired. As the first milestone draws near, the team puts in more and more hours in order to make the deadline. Once it is past, they again relax a bit before working toward the next milestone.

In an Agile project, when increments are short (such as every 2 weeks), if a team is used to pushing toward a deadline, they will be pushing all the time with no slow periods to compensate. This quickly leads to burnout and your best people will just quit because they can find other jobs. In addition, quality will suffer, which is a long term cost to the company. It also eventually has an impact on the schedule, because the more tired people are, the more mistakes they make, which then have to be fixed instead of spending the time working on new features.

Instead, an Agile team makes a reasonable estimate of the work they can complete in an increment. They will often plan on programming and testing about 32-35 hours a week, with the rest of the time taken up with a variety of meetings they are required to attend. This allows the team to keep working at a steady pace year after year without burning out and without quality suffering.

Sustainable pace is hard to do when managers keep pushing for more work in less time. I know of far too many companies that put programmers on salary and expect them to work 60 hours a week all the time. Over 30 years of research shows that you can do this for about 4 weeks, then productivity drops dramatically due to people being exhausted. What these companies get is a lot of mistakes, poor quality products, longer projects (to fix the mistakes made by tired people), and high turnover of staff compared to companies where people work a steady 40 hours a week.

Pair Programming

People have always asked a team mate for help when stuck on a problem. Pair programming formalizes that practice by having everyone program in pairs. That way the two programmers are constantly helping each other figure things out. But why stop pairing with programming? I pair for pretty much everything whenever possible. The work is completed faster and is superior to work I produce by myself.

In knowledge work, of which programming and writing books are two examples, it happens often that a person gets mentally stuck. Some people call it writer's block; some call it thinking. But work is not getting done at those times. Working together with another person almost removes the stuck points, and those that remain are much shorter. This is why a pair works so much faster than an individual and why the work is better.

A team I know paired everyone in their work, and changed the pairs frequently. A month into a 6 month 9 person project, a college hire joined the team and was paired over the next few months with everyone else in the team. Within 3 months, she was so knowledgeable about what the team was doing and how to do work at that company, and she was so productive, that people meeting her for the first time thought she had been working there for several years. Other college students hired at the same time were far behind her in just that 3 month period. And the project? Finished on-time and on-budget with more features and higher quality than comparable projects that did not encourage pairing.

Pair programming can be hard to implement because of how individuals are rewarded for their work. Many companies only reward for individual contributions and so there is no incentive for people to work together on a task. Their managers may discourage it because they do not know how to measure personal productivity when two people are working together. I have also found that many managers oppose doing it without even trying because they think it will slow the team down.

The easiest way to overcome objections is to find a manager who is willing to try pair programming on her project and measure the results. The best way is to let the team work for some time (maybe a month) as they usually do and measure productivity. Then have the team pair to do their programming for an equivalent time and again measure productivity. Then you have real proof if it will work or not inside your company and the cost of the experiment is low.

Section Four

The Agile Practices

God grant me the serenity to accept the things I cannot change, the courage to change the things I can, and the wisdom to know the difference.

- Reinhold Niebuhr

An Introduction to the Practices

I n prior sections I discussed practices that could be isolated within one department or division without requiring change to other parts of the company. These practices definitely can have a larger benefit in organizing work between departments or divisions, and can drive larger changes in the organization, but they do not have to be used that way.

The practices in this section will drive change in other parts of the company, including at least human resources, contracts, facilities, security, marketing, procurement, operations, and executives at all levels of the company. These are changes that affect the structures, relationships, metrics, and rewards of your company, and so may be very difficult or impossible to implement inside of large well-established companies that already have a functional corporate culture.

Depending on your company's culture, some of these practices may be very easy to implement requiring very little change, or perhaps the change is welcomed. In other companies, those same practices may be impossible to implement because the change is so radical. In addition, for that large of a change the benefits received may not be worth the cost, and the benefits may not even be considered beneficial to the company.

For each of the following practices, I'll describe the kind of corporate culture I typically see and discuss why that makes implementing the practice difficult. I'll also discuss what kind of corporate culture makes it easier to implement the practice. This will give you the information you need to determine if adopting this practice is feasible at your company.

Chapter 11

Co-location

C o-location refers to seating people together who are working on the same project or effort and typically also means they work on the same schedule. Co-location is a strong mitigation for the risk of problems due to poor communication between team members. When I speak of teams, I mean people who are collaborating to get a job done. If everyone is working completely individually, that is not a team for the purposes of this discussion.

Poor communication may seem like a small problem, but the actual productivity loss is at least 10%, and often much higher. Just think about how much information you miss when you are on the road, out sick, or on vacation. Now imagine how much you would miss if you were never physically in the office. Often the problems this causes are small, but sometimes this lack of communication leads to very large, expensive, and messy problems.

There are two primary advantages to co-location; it removes communication delays between team members and removes the problem of lack of communication. Instead of sending an email, text message, or instant message and waiting for a reply, the team member is able to talk with any other team member immediately. And since everyone is physically together, everyone learns about important information, especially information shared in informal conversation.

If you want the advantages of co-location, and you cannot physically co-locate team members, then virtual co-location can be an alternative if the team members work in nearby time zones. Some teams have made virtual co-location work using tools such as continuous online or video conferencing, chat rooms, telepresence work spaces, role play software (such as Second Life which lets people create personas and work together online), telepresence robots, and work schedules adjusted so that the team members are working at the same time (i.e. everyone works 9am – 5pm US Central time, no matter what time zone they are in). If the team members cannot mostly overlap their work days (6 hours or more when everyone is working at the same time), then virtual co-location is of limited use, and may not be worth the cost of the infrastructure to support it.

Another option for reducing the risks associated with poor communication or lack of communication is to mostly remove the need for collaboration between team members. Open source products take this approach. Open source products have rules, infrastructure support, and a small group of people who manage the infrastructure and enforce the rules. This mostly removes the need for the people working on the product to collaborate with each other. Because the need for collaboration is mostly removed there is no real need to co-locate. Practices that support this model include small well-defined work packages, a well-defined architecture, design by contract to reduce or eliminate the need for collaboration, and short increments to quickly find any problems or misunderstandings so they can be corrected immediately.

The highest risk situation from a communication perspective is to create one team made up of small groups in different locations in wide-spread time zones and expect the small groups to collaborate with each other. If you have this situation, the best approach to reduce risk is to co-locate people within each small group, then remove the need for the different small groups to collaborate with each other (or make that collaboration quite minimal).

Corporate Structures that Make Co-location Very Difficult or Expensive

Many companies have policies and procedures that make it difficult or expensive to co-locate teams. You may have teams with members in many different locations and so it is impossible for them to work in the same place. Many companies are adopting required work from home time. Team members may be far enough apart in time zones that it is not feasible for them to work at the same time.

If you are working at a US company that outsources a lot of work to India, and you have for example all the programmers in the US and all the testers in India, you may find it is not possible to remove the need for the team members to collaborate and the time zones are too far apart for virtual co-location to be very effective.

You may form a team for a project, then disband the team at the end of the project, thus requiring that people be moved to new co-location spaces every time they change projects. You may have individual people working on multiple projects at a time, so they need a different physical place to work for every team they are part of. Many roles work only some of a project lifecycle and so join a team for a time and then leave. You quickly run out of space for people to work because each person has multiple work spaces to accommodate all the teams he/she is part of.

If you create physical cubicles for each person, with workstations and telephones physically wired into a network, moving people around can be very expensive and time consuming. You may require facilities teams to do the physical moving of people, not allowing people to move themselves. In this situation, implementing co-location will quickly overwhelm the ability of your facilities teams to do the work of moving people.

Corporate Structures that Make Co-location Easier

You may already have policies and procedures that make co-location easier or less expensive to implement, or can relatively easily put them in place.

Perhaps everyone works on high-end laptops or tablets with really good wireless throughout the building. There are no desk telephones, everyone has a corporate smart phone for their telephone number and associated email, texting, and calendar services, and outlets and charging stations are easy to find.

Perhaps you remove assigned cubicles or workstations – every work location is set up so anyone can sit and start working. Office supplies and printers are kept in easy to find locations, it is very easy to set up to print to any printer, and someone is responsible for ensuring the supplies are stocked and the printers maintained.

To make it easy for people to move from place to place, you discourage people from storing "stuff" at work. You have an extensive company library (perhaps electronic or an online book service) so people do not need to have their own collection of books, journals, etc. stored at their desk. Information needed to work is electronic, backed up regularly, and easily accessible so people do not need to keep paper copies of historical project documents (for example) stored at their desks. Your people are encouraged to keep personal stuff such as awards or photos on their own smart phone, tablet, or cloud service.

Because of a lack of stuff to move, and lack of hard wired infrastructure, people can move themselves by simply picking up their electronic devices and walking to another location. You do not require facilities to construct the new space, then ask people to pack their stuff, then have facilities move them, then have people unpack their stuff every time they need to work with a new team.

While the actual work of your company is globally distributed, you may have a policy of requiring any particular group of people who have to work together to be within 2 or 3 time zones of each other so that they can feasibly have overlapping work schedules. You provide the ability for anyone to easily and at any time virtually co-locate.

Dividing work into independent work packages (one of the Big Three Management Practices) facilitates distributed teams because you can send different work packages to different physical locations for implementation without requiring much interaction between people working on the different work packages. The people working on one work package only need to be co-located with each other, not with people working on other work packages.

While these things look pretty extensive, a lot of them are changes to hardware which you are probably considering anyway. It is only money. Harder to change will be getting people to give up personal workspaces and possibly it will be hard to create teams whose members are within 2 or 3 time zones. Giving up personal workspaces will be hard if your culture is one where each person has "his" or "her" desk. A lot of people are uncomfortable giving up a "permanent space" where they work. These are somewhat difficult changes, but not at all the hardest thing to make co-location work.

The Surprising Thing That Makes Co-location Really Difficult

Now that you have made it relatively easy for people to co-locate, can they actually do it? If most individuals are working on multiple projects or work efforts at the same time, it is almost certainly impossible for a whole project team or other work group to be able to find a regular time when they can all sit together. Every effort they are part of is trying to do the same thing, so some number of people on any team will need to be in more than one place at the same time (which is impossible). If you think about holding a weekly project status meeting, you already know that some people will be there every other week because they have another project status meeting at the same time. That is much less time than we would hope to have a team co-locate and it is already not possible.

Remember the goal of co-location is to remove communication delays and avoid missed communications. It is much easier to do this if each person is dedicated to one effort – one project, one team, one workgroup. See the section on dedication for more information on that practice.

This section assumes you cannot dedicate people to one effort at a time but do want to use co-location to solve some kinds of communication problems. The suggestions below are based on the idea of dividing work up into work packages that can be implemented in a short time (typically less than a week) by 2-3 people.

Try co-locating a lot of people. Create a large open space where you have up to 100 people seated. These people would all be working on related work – for example on different projects in the same program, on the same asset, or in the same domain – and anyone they need to work with is within sight. Whenever a person needs to talk with a colleague she can walk over to his desk.

In this area you have plenty of places with desks or tables, white boards, and supplies where people can gather together when more than 2 or 3 people need to collaborate. Casual unscheduled areas work better in this regard than meeting rooms because meeting rooms have schedules which get filled, often by people saving space for meetings that never happen, or by people outside the area who cannot find meeting space in their own area. It is easy to share information through casual conversation because the people who work together see each other throughout the day.

If some people are not physically in the building but can overlap work hours, many teams solve this by having web conferencing software running all day so everyone can see everyone else on a second monitor or using telepresence robots for the people who are not physically in the office (again logged in all day). You might think that the team members can just call the person at home or other location as needed, but that rarely happens in real life. The co-located team members just forget to call those who are not physically present.

This approach works because all the work is divided into work packages that are small enough for 2-3 people to implement in a week or less (and often just 1-2 days). They can focus that amount of time to working just with each other before moving to the next work package. If you have made it possible for people to casually co-locate as described above, then you can let the team members organize their schedules and physical space based on the needs of the work they are currently doing. These small workgroups quickly form and dissolve as needed. Other work may be completed by individuals who do not need to collaborate to get the job done.

This approach obviously requires a lot of communication with the various managers of the different projects and work efforts to determine which things will go much better with co-location and of those, which have priority if there is a conflict. This approach asks the team members themselves to be involved in how they organize to do work and requires a lot of cooperation among managers. This also requires there to be plenty of space available with desks, whiteboards, and supplies so it is easy for people to find an area to casually co-locate for a time.

If you are forming teams whose members are over 3 time zones apart, then those teams will gain very little benefit from trying to co-locate compared to the cost. In that case, to avoid the communication issues with distributed teams, look into something like the open source model that removes most of the need for the team members to collaborate.

Chapter 12

Dedication

Dedication refers to having people work on one team at a time and one thing at a time. Dedication is a strong mitigation for the risk of the work being too expensive. This practice helps people to focus their work which makes them far more efficient than dividing their time between multiple efforts. Over 90 years of research has been done on multi-tasking and all of that research shows that multi-tasking is far less efficient than doing one task to completion, then doing the next task to completion and so on. The advantage to dedication is to greatly reduce non-productive time.

The cost of working on multiple teams is not very high when the work is purely physical. It is when the work is done with the mind that the cost of working on multiple efforts at the same time grows dramatically. If people are assigned to 2 or 3 different teams at a time, changing the model to create permanent teams who focus on one work package at a time can save 25-60% of the cost of developing the solution depending on the nature of the different projects. 25-60% of the project schedule and budget is the cost of switching back and forth between 2 - 3 projects every day, every week. If you focus people on one effort at a time, that is the amount of time that will become available for productive work.

This cost does not even consider the cost of forming a new team and the cost of disbanding them. That cost is estimated at 3-9% of the total project budget due to the cost of moving people to sit together, setting up, changing, or removing software on their workstations, getting them access to servers, hosts, rooms, buildings, or people that will need to be accessed, and the lost productive time spent learning to work together.

There is also a management cost of having to spend time looking for a project to assign someone to. Staffing may need to ebb and flow as you have more demands for certain kinds of work at certain times of year. By keeping teams together, it is easier to move to a steady state, a steady rhythm of work, which simplifies staffing.

I have worked on dedicated teams and I have worked on multiple projects at the same time. It is clear to everyone with similar experience, that we get far more done in less time in dedicated teams. Research, including very recent research in modern companies, shows exactly the same result. When you choose to put individuals on multiple efforts at the same time you are increasing the cost of the work due to increasing the amount of time it takes to switch between projects / tasks. You may have good reasons for not dedicating people to one project at a time, but then you need to look for other ways to reduce cost.

Corporate Structures that Make Dedication Very Difficult or Expensive

Companies that create centers of excellence or silos of skills and matrix people onto projects are set up the opposite of creating permanent teams. Matrix managers do not want to "give up" their people to stay on one team. There is the question of who is the manager of the people on the team. There will be problems if different people on the same team have different managers.

If a person is highly specialized, there may not be enough work on one team to keep that person busy. If your job descriptions and promotion practices are such that people are rewarded for specializing, then you may not be able to keep everyone on the team working all the time in their specialty. Due to a particular mix of skill sets, you may not be able to find enough appropriate work to keep a particular team busy in any given year.

Dedicating people to teams will cause changes in the portfolio process. If you are accustomed to starting multiple projects at once because every stakeholder wants to know you are working on their project now, you will have real issues trying to convince some people to wait for their projects to start, even though everything will complete faster if teams are working on one project at a time. You may be able to mitigate this by creating work packages for every project then streaming work packages from different projects to the same team. They work on one work package at a time, perhaps for 1 week, then the next work package can come from a different project, so every project gets some work within a month. You may run into issues with not spending money fast enough compared to the budget.

If all of your work is accounted for through projects, keeping teams together may cause problems for accounting. While it is easy to see what a particular team costs, it may be more challenging to allocate their costs against specific projects. Companies that use dedicated teams often do not have projects. Instead they structure the work around assets and releases. This is a very different accounting structure than reporting against projects.

Corporate Structures that Make Dedication Easier

Large companies that are structured around assets or programs find it relatively easy to dedicate people to an asset or program. The asset or program is funded for the year, which determines how many people are on the team. The team works toward release deadlines from a queue of work that is typically created and managed by a management team including business and technical leaders. Asset or program teams tend to be large – 30-100 people – but they do not all try to work together. Instead small work groups form within the team to work on a particular work package. The asset or program team has to be big enough to keep the specialists busy, but small enough everyone knows everyone else (this is the key to small work groups being able to start working together quickly without the time delays of team building).

To make this approach work, work packages have to describe work that is as independent as possible (one of the Big Three Management Practices). Small work groups ebb and flow as needed to complete the work of each work package. Release dates are used to coordinate the work within the asset or program. Because the asset or program team is large you can have all necessary skills within the team and not have to go outside the team for specialist resources (or very rarely so).

If you cannot change the funding model away from projects to assets or programs, you can set up a management team between the funding source and the implementation teams. The job of the management team is to make it look like work is implemented by project but to manage the people doing the implementing as a program or asset team.

The management team takes in all the projects, divides them into work packages, and creates a consolidated queue of work packages (one of the Big Three Management Practices). This management team treats all the implementers for all the projects as one big team, and assigns work packages to work groups created from that larger team. Since you still have to account for time against a specific project, the work packages could be tagged or color coded to indicate the project each one belongs to. Then for each work package, the people implementing it know where to charge their time. As new projects need to start, the managers divide them into work packages and add them to the queue.

The managers have to keep careful track of schedules and budgets of projects by combining the schedule and cost information of the work packages that make up the projects. The management team is responsible for reporting status to the stakeholders of the various projects. This approach requires a lot of cooperation between the managers of the people who implement your solutions.

In some cases you may have enough related projects that require a relatively small set of skills to keep a team of maybe 15 people together for the year. The team does one project, then their manager keeps the team together and gives them another project to work on. This approach assumes that the 15 or so people have all or most of the skills needed to complete a stream of projects over the year. You can use a visiting specialist model to fill in the few skills the team does not have to complete the project.

Dedication is also easier if your company policies encourage people to develop broad skill sets. The more specialized your people become, the harder it is to dedicate them to a team because there is not enough work within one team or project for those specialized skills. Because people with broad skill sets (sometimes called generalists) can do many different things you will usually be able to create relatively small teams with complete skill sets. (See the section on Generalizing Specialists for more information on this practice.)

The Surprising Thing That Makes Dedication Really Difficult

If your company values specialists and rewards people for becoming even more specialized over time, dedication will be very difficult to achieve. In this kind of company, you see silos of specialties. Because of the size of the company, there are many different kinds of work and many different specialties are needed to do that work. The end result is that typically any one person has a limited amount of work that he or she can do on any one project (except your least experienced people, the college hires who have not yet begun to specialize).

The approach you see recommended in the Agile community is instead of creating projects and assigning people to the project, create teams of 7 plus or minus 2 people where each team has all the skills needed to do the work it is assigned and then keep streaming work to the team. Then you are asked to leave those teams together over the long term. To be able to do this, each person must have a broad skill set or you create these teams in situations where the people only require a limited skill set to do the work. For example, you may be able to create these small dedicated teams in a company that only produces mobile apps or in a division of your company that only produces mobile apps independently of other work being done.

If your company values specialists and you want to take the traditional Agile approach, this will have a high impact on your organizational structures that deal with how people are assigned to work, what they are expected to do, who they report to, how they are evaluated, and how they are promoted. Job classifications, job descriptions, and promotion sequences will change. You may not have matrix organizations anymore or matrix managers.

Even worse than this, the people you have working for you already know what to expect in terms of how to progress in their careers, and now you are proposing to change the entire model. This will make a lot of people very unhappy. If you do not make those changes, and the job descriptions and classifications continue to reward for specialization, you cannot expect people to work as generalists and stay with your company for very long.

You will almost certainly run into problems with not being able to meet productivity metrics for a while as people learn new skills. You will have issues around what to do with people who have highly specialized skills and how to ensure every team has all the skills it needs to do the work it needs to do. You may run into security issues if more people than previously need to access secure systems. You may also run into issues from operations when they want to "borrow" someone off a project team to do some maintenance work or to fix an urgent bug.

This is why large asset or program teams as described above are recommended for large companies because you can achieve dedication to the larger team without causing such a huge impact on your workforce. There are changes in how the work is managed, but that is easier than changing from a specialist to a generalist model.

Without dedication, your projects will be at least 25-60% higher cost than equivalent teams who dedicate. This is due to the frequency and complexity of task switching. If you really cannot make change to dedicate people to their work, you will be hard-pressed to find a way to compensate for that loss.

Chapter 13

Teaming

Teaming is an approach to organizing a group of people to get work done. Teaming mitigates the risks of going over budget, over schedule, and having poor quality results. While many companies and people say they work in "teams" this is actually rarely the case. If a group of people is working as a team, they are actually daily collaborating on doing work together. This is very different from a group of people who divide up the work then each person works on his/her own part independently.

When people see themselves as part of a team, whatever work needs to be done, someone steps up to take care of it. They use the word "we" a lot when describing what they do. When people see themselves as individuals, they tend to do exactly what they are "supposed" to do and no more. You hear them say things like "that is not my job". They use the word "I" a lot.

For the purposes of this discussion, a team can be as small as 2 or as large as about 15 to be really effective. The advantage to teaming is greatly increased output (or faster time to market) with far higher quality compared to the same number of people working as individuals.

People will organize their work the way you reward them. No matter how much you talk about teamwork, if you have individual performance reviews, only review the work that meets the official job description, rank employees in terms of performance, and compare them to each other when considering rewards, you will get individual contributors, not teams. With individual contributors, people work mostly alone, and you review and reward the work of individuals. With teamwork, people together as a team, and your review and reward the work of the team.

A lot of research over many decades shows that actual teams (people who daily collaborate in their work) far outperform the work of the same number of people working as individuals. Far outperform means the team typically does twice the work (or more) as the same number of people working mostly individually. I have been privileged a number of times in my career to work as a member of a real team. Not only was the output far more than double the work of an equivalent number of individuals, the quality of the work was far higher as well. It was also a lot more fun and hugely satisfying.

A big advantage of teaming is the company no longer depends on superstars to make it all work, thus removing the risk of depending on a small number of individuals to keep the company running. Over time you will get more consistent performance throughout the organization, and a highly motivated, happy work force.

You might think this only works with "A" players. It turns out that your highest performing teams are very likely composed of quite ordinary individuals. Working as a true team raises everyone's game. Statistically any team could surprise you and turn out to be great. As an example, I will point to a company in Ann Arbor, Michigan called Menlo Innovations. For 15 years this company, which develops software for corporate clients, has consistently hired ordinary programmers who were good team players. They have also consistently produced products for their customers that outperform the competition in the marketplace and cost much less to develop than the competition spends. For 15 years they have proved that the winning formula is ordinary programmers + outstanding teamwork.

Corporate Structures that Make Teaming Very Difficult or Expensive

There are a number of things about large companies that prevent real teamwork. Teams need time to develop into a cohesive working unit. Any military knows how to create a team and they do it all the time in boot camp: put people together 24 hours a day in a high stress situation with a common enemy (the drill sergeant). You don't need to go that far to create teams, but you will not get teams to form if you put people on multiple projects at the same time. You will not get teams to form if the members cannot co-locate at least in time using virtual co-location tools.

I have had people insist to me they were part of teams where everyone was located in different places in different time zones. After some investigation I discovered that there was no real teamwork; with some small effort to decide who worked on what, everyone worked as an individual. Their results made it clear; they did not have exceptional output, speed, or quality. When I reviewed the work of these "teams" I found it to be just adequate.

Other things that block teamwork are how jobs and hierarchies of jobs are described, and performance goals and rewards based on individual effort. You rank people against each other to determine who gets raises. When you mentor young people you advise them to always make sure the boss knows what they individually are accomplishing to promote their career. These practices encourage people to work alone, typically in a cubicle or office, to hide what they are doing from others, and to take credit for good work even if someone else did it.

In an effort to create teams, many companies will ask the managers to create teams. The members themselves have no choice who they get to work with, and will get stuck with low performers, people who are so unpleasant no one wants to work with them, and outstanding individual contributors who go off on their own and don't talk to anyone. All of these people will prevent a team from ever forming. Morale in this situation is low and people do not do their best work. They will tough it out until they can get into a better situation (maybe at another company).

Managers are afraid to let people form their own teams because then they have to deal with the "problem children" that no one wants. Some of the "problem children" are being protected by powerful sponsors who are unhappy when their buddy is not getting "the rewards he or she deserves". HR or Legal may be afraid that someone who is not working out will sue the company for unfair treatment and thus these departments will prevent you from allowing teams to choose their own members.

This individual reward system suits people who are very competitive and sell themselves well. Recent research suggests that this system works well for Baby Boomers who were generally raised to be competitive.

Corporate Structures that Make Teaming Easier

Companies who have real teams are structured to enable teams to form. The members of the team are co-located in time and space. The members of the team all focus on one work package at a time.

The team self-organizes based on the work to be done. People are not locked into specific described roles; everyone is a team member. Senior people do not always lead; sometimes a junior team member has the vision and provides the leadership. Leadership and other roles shift based on the needs of the work. There are team measurements of performance that help the team understand what is expected and how well they are doing. Some companies reward teams by giving bonuses when the team saves the company money through practices such as delivering to market early or delivering higher quality code that is less expensive to maintain.

An individual's performance goals are set based on how to increase the person's value to the company and they include how well this person contributes to the team. Raises are based on how well the person did against goals, and thus his/her increased value to the company, not how well he or she did compared to others. If everyone has done really well this year, everyone gets a raise or bonus. There is no artificial bell curve to adhere to.

Working closely with management, the team selects its own members and removes people who are not working out for any reason. Management suggests rotations between teams to help people learn new skill sets, enhance knowledge of underlying systems, and get a chance to work with more people. This system rewards team players. Competition is between teams, and since people rotate between teams, it tends to be gracious competition, where competition exists not to put others down, but to help everyone strive to be even better.

This system rewards people who are cooperative and work very well with others. Current research suggests that this system works well for Millennials who were generally raised to be cooperative.

The Surprising Thing That Makes Teaming Really Difficult

In most large companies I have been in, competition is a way of life from top to bottom. Not only is it accepted, but there are large numbers of people who thrive in this environment. They understand the model, they know how to make it work for them. A widespread change to a teaming model is certain to fail. If it did succeed, you would lose a huge percentage of your workforce, especially among the most senior people who would no longer know how to work at your company.

You can add a teamwork factor into the individual performance goals of people who are working on teams. At the same time, if you allow the team to select its own members, then your high performing individual contributors will not mind the new teamwork factor because they will choose to work with other successful people. Thus by helping the team succeed, they also succeed, and they have a lot of fun working with other successful people.

Where you run into trouble with this approach is when a team is forced to have members who underperform. The rest of the team will feel like they have to do their work and the underperforming members' work so they can have a good teamwork value for their yearly review. This causes a lot of resentment among the people who are doing the actual work and they will eventually rebel.

There probably is not a need to have everyone work in teams. Some people just do not work well with others (including perhaps some of your top performers) and trying to force them to will probably lead them to quit. It is far easier to start with some teams, and over time add more teams if it makes sense to do so. You might still have some lone performers even if most people work on teams.

For the best results, work toward allowing the teams to choose their own members. The team members should work closely with management to set them up. Managers also have a place in helping the teams plan rotations of members between teams. This allows team members an opportunity to work with a new set of people and acquire new skills. Managers should be involved if the team cannot address some problems, for example human resources may require management to be involved if a person is not able to work in a team environment.

Most places I have worked practice benign neglect when it comes to teams. If a group of people form a team and things are working well, they tend to be left alone. One company I worked for really wanted the advantage of teams. They did internal interviews to discover people within the company who naturally formed teams around themselves. This company also looked for managers who valued teams and teamwork more than superstars. These managers created teams with the natural teamers and let the other people continue to shine as individual contributors working for managers who appreciated their way of working. It worked rather well since neither model was positioned as being somehow better than the other. This approach allowed everyone to play to their strengths.

If you form true teams around your most critical areas where speed and quality are the most important, you gain the benefit of teams where it really matters without making widespread (and potentially very expensive) changes to your organization.

Chapter 14

Generalizing Specialists

S pecialists are people who gain deep knowledge and experience in one area of expertise. Generalists are people who gain broad knowledge and experience in many areas of expertise. In their area of expertise, specialists are generally more efficient than a generalist doing the same job. Specialists are limited to doing work in their specialty. Generalists can be put to work on anything that needs to be done.

You cause problems in efficiency, quality, and timeliness of deliveries if you have all specialists or all generalists. If you have all specialists, you have the kinds of problems the specialists cannot find because the problems occur in a combination of specialties. If you have all generalists, you have solutions that will not be found because the generalists do not know those solutions are possible. You may end up with less optimal solutions because the generalists do not have enough knowledge to find the optimal solutions.

Many companies find that generalizing specialists solve both problems neatly; they are specialists in some area, but have acquired enough skill in one or more other areas to be able to work in those areas as well. A generalizing specialist tends to work in his/her specialty and does other kinds of work when there is no specialty work to do or when the other work is more important. Developing generalizing specialists mitigates the risk of having only one person (or maybe two) who can do a particular kind of work and removes work blockages and slow downs due to the unavailability of the specialists.

I know a number of outstanding generalizing specialists who have saved their companies a lot of money over the years or fixed problems no one else could. One generalizing specialist I know is a genius at mechanical systems, but also understands electrical, firmware, and software systems very well. He has worked in all these areas in his career. An outstanding example of the value of a generalizing specialist was the time when a group of electrical and firmware engineers came to him with a bug they had been unable to fix for 6 months. Within one day he had found the bug, created, and tested the solution. This kind of thing happened often in his career, and his employers valued him for that reason. He has been fortunate to find employers who recognize that he can contribute more than his specialty.

The disadvantage to generalizing specialists is that they are less efficient working in their secondary fields than a specialist would be doing the same work. The generalizing specialist mentioned above does a great job with basic electrical engineering work (not his specialty), but when the need is for specialized circuitry, it takes him longer to do the job than it would for an electrical engineer. This is because he has to research what he does not know and he will make mistakes that a specialist would not. The work is done within an acceptable time period with quite good quality, and so he is asked to do such work when an electrical engineering specialist is not available. Sometimes his boss will wait for the specialist and sometimes not depending on the urgency of the work.

When putting teams together to work on products, having generalizing specialists as team members means you can very likely have all the skills within the team to get the job done. While they may be somewhat less efficient at some of their work, this loss is made up when the team does not have to wait for a specialist to become available, nor do they have delays due to having to explain to an outside specialist what needs to be done.

Innovation often comes from generalizing specialists. This is because they look at a problem from multiple perspectives and frequently come up with novel solutions that would never occur to the specialists. There is a new role in marketing called Growth Hacker or Growth Engineer.

These are programmers who cross train in marketing. They are creating tools that traditional marketers have never thought of because these programmers know what is possible to do with software and the marketing experts do not.

Corporate Structures that Make Generalizing Specialists Very Difficult or Expensive

The big things that block people from becoming generalists or generalizing specialists are job descriptions, families of jobs, and promotion paths that describe increasing levels of specialization. Then individual performance goals and evaluations are based on those descriptions which makes it possible for people to advance in their career only if they specialize.

Within a culture of specialization it is very difficult to get people to do anything other than specialize. Generalists are almost never interviewed for positions at your company because your application systems are all set up to scan resumes based on your specialized job descriptions. There will always be some people who want to broaden their skill set, and they will most likely leave your company because they do not see a career path for themselves. Those who are left are those who know well how to succeed in a specialist environment. In this environment, generalists are not hired and generalists are not grown.

Specialists will be jealous of their standing as a specialist and will not be very interested in a change away from that model. Unless you change the company reward structures, your specialists will not be very willing to share their knowledge with others or cross train in new skills.

Human Resources (HR) will not be at all happy with needing to rewrite job descriptions, and rewrite and train managers in the directions on how to set performance goals and conduct performance reviews. HR will be especially unhappy with the idea that human beings will have to do more work to review resumes.

Managers will not like having to learn a new way to reward employees based on encouraging broader skill sets. Since managers or other senior personnel will likely be those who have to review the larger set of resumes looking for candidates, they will not be happy about the additional time this takes.

Another way generalists are blocked is that the best jobs go to those who work in a center of excellence. Sometimes everyone works for some center of excellence. Some examples of centers of excellence we have seen include Business Analysis, Architecture, Database, Programmers, Compliance, Risk, and Project Management. When that kind of expertise is needed on a team or project, you "borrow" a specialist from the center of excellence to do the work. There may be little or no interaction with other people working on the team or project. People in the center of excellence tend to spend their time with each other, becoming more and more specialized and less aware of what other people do. It is how they are rewarded and so it is how they work.

Security may have set up silos of access to systems based on specialties and be unwilling to let larger numbers of people have access to those systems. The managers of the centers of excellence are now reduced to leading the guilds which may not be enough to keep them interested. Most centers of excellence are understaffed so you can be sure that the specialists are already busy. Until more people cross-train in at least the fundamentals of the specialist's knowledge, you cannot move the specialists full-time onto teams. You also have to figure out what the guilds do and who runs them, creating possibly new roles and new kinds of work.

Examine where you really need to have centers of excellence. Some small number of specialties will still need a separate organization, such as Legal. It does not make sense to put a lawyer full time on a software delivery team because there is an occasional opinion needed, nor can you really cross train others in all the legal knowledge. A knowledge base of common legal answers might help ease the load on the lawyers though, so that their time is used for the less common situations.

150

Given all these changes, moving from a culture that promotes specialization to a model of generalizing specialists or a model of adding generalist roles to your organization is a really big task.

Corporate Structures that Make Generalizing Specialists Easier

A company that encourages generalizing specialists will form teams with broad knowledge and skills. Some team members will be true generalists, others will be specialists who have cross-trained in additional disciplines. Specialists are not tucked away in centers of excellence, but rather are full-time members of teams like everyone else. To enable coordination within the specialty, a company may have guilds or chapters that meet regularly (perhaps once a month) to share information or training related to the specialty. There may be a need to form short lived teams of specialists for a particular task, such as updating recommended processes and procedures. Instead of specialists being employed by the center of excellence and loaned to teams, the specialists are employed by the teams and loaned to the guild or chapter to coordinate with other specialists.

Job descriptions and career paths encourage specialists to broaden their skills. Performance goals and evaluations include those that reward gaining skills in new areas. Instead of relying on automated systems to do a keyword search based on a job description to find job candidates, resumes are reviewed by people who can evaluate different mixes of skill sets to find good candidates for a job.

The company has a culture of continuous improvement and encouraging people to try new things. This can take the form of reimbursement for education even if it does not directly relate to the person's current job, paid time for volunteer work, an allocation of some percent of the employee's time to work on anything that interests him or her, and some variation of suggestion box as just a few examples.

The Surprising Thing That Makes Generalizing Specialists Really Difficult

The one thing that makes creating generalists really difficult is a corporate culture of fear of failure. In this situation, there is too much risk for everyone in having generalists. It is too risky for a person to generalize because there may be work he or she does not do as well as a specialist, or this person may in fact fail in a task because of a lack of specialized knowledge. It is too risky for management to encourage people to try new things (and thus become generalists over time) because people trying new things will likely have some failures. If failure is not allowed, then there is also no room for growth, change, and innovation.

This one thing is very hard to overcome. You will find there are a lot of things within your company that make people fear failure. They may fear the impact on their career progression, loss of a job, loss of status, and even embarrassment. Changing a culture from punishing failure to treating it as an opportunity for growth may be a very long term change over an entire generation.

If you cannot move your company to a culture of generalizing specialists, you need to find other ways to reduce the time that teams have to wait for a specialist to become available. A traditional approach is to create a library or knowledge store of fundamental information, standards, and guidelines so the most common needs are satisfied by self-service. This information might be common legal answers, guidelines for updating a database, or architectural standards for just a few examples.

A mechanism to reduce the risk of having a very small amount of people who have some specialist knowledge is to create guilds for the different specialties. This does not require changes to your existing corporate structures except for adding guild meetings to the calendar. Anyone interested in the specialty should be allowed and encouraged to attend, not just the existing specialists. This is because part of the purpose of the guild is to share the knowledge with more people.

Chapter 15

Common Ownership of an Asset

With common ownership of asset, anyone can potentially work on anything that needs to be done to that asset. There are rules and guidance set up to avoid inconsistent changes, and typically an owner of the rules and guidance. The rules and guidance may include things such as a vision or architecture for the asset as it is today, a vision for the future development of the asset, rules on testing along with suites of tests, quality standards, guidelines for acceptance of changes or updates, and infrastructure that helps implementers coordinate their work.

Open source products are developed with this kind of model. It enables teams or individuals all over the world to work on the same product with minimal need for coordination. It also makes it easy for new people to join at any time, or current people to leave, without disruption, loss of knowledge, or the need for handoffs. Within a company, this practice provides a powerful means for distributing work across the enterprise and a means to smooth out the natural ebbs and flows of the work. It also greatly reduces the risk of dependency on a small number of people who are the only ones who know how your products and other capital assets work.

You might think that having only one person know the asset is just a problem for startups. In fact, it is very common for one or two people who started with the company to be the only people who know how their product works. I always advise these companies to get more people knowledgeable about the product as fast as possible because they are literally risking the whole company on one or two people.

But I have seen exactly the same thing in Fortune 500 companies.

In one company where I worked, the company was maintaining a vital system on a mainframe. It worked quite well, but management wanted to stop using mainframes. The head developer and owner of this system had never learned any programming language but COBOL and did not know how to work on any system except a mainframe. Over the years, he had prevented anyone from learning how the system worked and he did not document how it worked in any way. The company was completely dependent on him to keep this very important system running. He blocked all efforts to move the system off the mainframe thus guaranteeing he would continue to have a high prestige job (without having to learn anything new) until his planned retirement a few years from that time.

I have seen this over and over in companies large and small. It is a technique that is lucrative in many ways for the owner of the system as long as he or she does not mind being interrupted on vacation with emergencies at work.

To make common ownership of asset work does require creating infrastructure that supports centralized storage of asset information. Many companies store information project by project, but that makes it essentially impossible to find all the information concerning a particular asset. Instead, everyone needs access to all information about the asset such as the vision and/or architecture of the asset, plans for the future, design information showing how the asset is constructed or works, process documents, and tests that proves the asset works as designed. In addition to the asset (whether it is code, hardware, other physical devices, reports, or processes), everyone who works on it is responsible for keeping the documentation up-to-date.

With common ownership you might think there is no accountability. If everyone owns it, no one owns it. Instead it is the opposite. Every person is responsible and accountable for his/her work on the asset. If someone makes a change that causes problems, that person is responsible for fixing the problems. When there are one or two owners of an asset, they are typically responsible for the vision and provide limited access to other people to do the actual maintenance of the asset. Then when there are problems they can claim that the problems were caused by one or more implementers or testers or it is the user's mistake or there was a change to the server that caused it. Everyone blames someone else, so no one ends up being accountable.

Corporate Structures that Make Common Ownership Very Difficult or Expensive

One of the biggest reasons that it is hard to have common ownership of your assets is that the information about the asset is not documented or the documentation is too hard to find. When the information about the asset is inside people's heads, it limits who can work on the asset to those who already know it or those who can find the people who know it. This situation arises for a variety of reasons: information is stored project by project, information is deleted due to corporate data retention policies, and information about the asset is not created (time pressure or wanting to keep anyone else from knowing how it works).

When you store information project by project, then in order for someone to find out how an asset works, that person has to know (or find out) all the projects that touched that asset over many years. Then that person has to find all the project repositories and sort through the files looking for information that is relevant to the asset. This is so time consuming that most of the time the person looking for information will give up and will instead try to find people who have worked on the asset to interview them to find the information. That assumes that the people who worked on the asset remember the necessary details and still work for your company. Because this process is so time consuming, it is just easier to have the same people work on the asset all the time. Just hope they do not go to work for a competitor or retire taking all that knowledge with them (and yes I have seen exactly that happen many, many times).

Sometimes information about the asset cannot be found due to corporate data retention policies. Many companies have policies to delete project information after some amount of time, maybe 3 years, maybe 7. Asset information should not be subject to those policies, but if you are storing information project by project, then likely your asset information is getting deleted. You may think it is not relevant after so long, but I know of many systems that are in use after 30 and even 40 years. There are parts of those systems that have not needed attention for a very long time and so the projects that did those updates have long been deleted from your systems. And if those parts of the system do need attention, it is quite likely that the people who originally worked on the system no longer work for your company.

Sometimes the information about the asset was never created. This is often due to the pressure to complete a project. Since the focus is on releasing the asset for use, documentation is seen as not very important and so it is often not created. There are also situations where someone does not want the asset documented because then that person has a guaranteed job maintaining that asset. No one else knows how it works, so no one else can take over maintaining it.

Sometimes you cannot have more than one or two people working on an asset because it is so poorly structured that it takes someone new a very long time to understand it and there is a high risk that a new person will cause something to go wrong (through lack of understanding). This situation is typically combined with a lack of any kinds of tests that can verify the asset works correctly making it very easy to inadvertently break something. I had one group tell me that it was impossible to get a new person up to speed on the asset in less than two years. Yes years. That is not a typo. This discouraged management from moving anyone out of that asset group and from moving anyone new in.

Other issues may come from security. Security people like to create silos of information to control exactly who has access to what in order to decrease risks such as fraud or stealing corporate information. Sometimes this has to be done, for example in cases where legally you must restrict access to personal protected information or where national security requires certain clearances be held before a person can have access to the information. These cases are not really all that common. The consequences are that for someone to get access to new information they have to request that access. This causes some amount of delay and additional work for security. In the worst case I have seen, access to systems and assets was turned on at the start of every project and turned off at the end, unless the person was just starting a new project in the same systems. So of course the same people worked in the same systems all the time.

Corporate Structures that Make Common Ownership Easier

Companies that encourage common ownership of assets create centralized repositories of asset information. In the best cases, these repositories are very easy to access and are maintained using tools such as wikis. Less ideal are tools which require accounts and logins to be created before the information can be accessed. If everyone was set up with an account that would be fine, but unfortunately it tends to be done on an "as needed" basis, there is typically a delay of several days to get access, and the person asking for it will tend to default to finding someone to ask rather than get access for him/her self to either read or update the information.

This repository is not subject to corporate data retention policies. It will exist as long as the asset is in use. Updating the repository is a serious responsibility of everyone who changes the asset. This responsibility is not allowed to be "forgotten" in the push to deliver a new release. Managers are also responsible for ensuring the repository is kept up-to-date.

Each asset does have a person (or small group of people) who is responsible overall for the asset. But their role is to provide direction, to keep the information about the asset up-to-date and accessible, and to create the policies and procedures that enable common ownership of the asset. The asset owners also ensure that people who are new to working on the asset get the information and education they need to do that work. You know you have done it right when no one calls an asset owner on their vacation (holiday) to deal with an emergency. There are plenty of people who can handle the problem.

Management encourages sharing of information and assists people in moving around to work on different assets and systems so more people gain knowledge of the company's assets. This practice mitigates the risk of the company depending on a very small number of people to run the business.

Good design of assets is measured and rewarded, making it relatively easy for new people to learn about the asset and how it works. There are suites of appropriate tests that ensure that when changes are made to the asset it is not broken.

Finally, security silos are only created when it really is necessary to do so. Even in those cases, the number of people with access to the information is large enough that the loss of one or two is not a problem.

The Surprising Thing That Makes Common Ownership Really Difficult

It would seem that organizing work as a series of projects supports the idea of common ownership. After all, whoever is working on the project is working on the asset and that changes over time. But actually the opposite is true. In this situation, no one feels ownership for the asset.

Project success is typically measured by on time and on budget. This fosters a short term focus on getting the work of the project done, not on doing the right thing for enabling large numbers of people to work on the asset. When the focus is on getting projects completed, teams are not motivated to maintain centralized asset documentation because it takes time out of a typically too short schedule and it does not benefit this project team. Updating documentation is the last thing a project team will do and when they run out of time (which almost always happens), the asset documentation is not updated.

Another issue is that the team is already asked to maintain required project documentation. This is something they and their manager are directly rewarded for doing, so it benefits them to do it. It is easy in that situation to forget to look to another repository for the asset documentation and to update it. The manager might say it is important to update the asset documents but I have not yet seen a case where there were any negative consequences for failing to update the asset documents. The opposite is true. If the asset documents are updated at the expense of updating project documents, then the team gets in trouble. So there is no motivation to update the asset documentation.

The focus on project success in many companies also means that there is a lack of quality standards or a lack of enforcement of quality standards. The project team is measured on delivering on time and budget and not on quality. Therefore quality also suffers. This is a quite well-known case throughout software development in companies large and small throughout the world. When you focus on deadlines, quality suffers. When the quality is poor, it makes it very difficult for the next team to work on the asset. This often leads to the case of having a small number of people do all the work on the asset because it is too hard for anyone else to learn it.

Project focus usually means there is no centralized repository of asset documentation. When someone wants to know how the asset is designed, then that person has to find someone who has worked on the asset or has to find the project repositories that have information on what that project did. This is very time consuming, so again tends to lead to having a very small number of people always work on the asset because no one else has time to find the information they need to work on it.

The reason all of this is bad is that over time your company will depend on a very small number of people to maintain your assets, which are the lifeblood of your company. When those people retire or leave for other reasons, you have no one left who knows your assets and systems. When work needs to be done, there is no one to do it. The cost of fixing the problem then is quite high compared to making sure you have a lot of people in your company who can do the necessary work.

I have worked with a number of companies who were quite panicked at losing some of their senior engineers and tried in the last couple of weeks before the engineers left to get other people up to speed on complicated assets. Sometimes this has not been possible, and the company had to unexpectedly create a replacement asset. Sometimes the company convinced the people who were retiring to set up a consulting contract at a much higher salary than they had been making before they left. This "solved" the problem only in the short term, because at some point those retired people will no longer be available to do the work.

Chapter 16

Agile Metrics for Progress

I n Agile, the fundamental measure of progress is regular demonstrations of functional solutions. This mitigates the risks of delivering the wrong thing, being late, and going over budget. It also removes the problem of 90% complete, but 90% still left to do.

We keep implementation cycles short – typically 2-3 weeks. It is hard to come very close to an accurate estimate of 6 months or several years of work. It is relatively easy to accurately estimate 2-3 weeks of work. You know exactly what you will be spending and what will be delivered in a 2-3 week period. At that end of the 2-3 weeks, you can take delivery of the solution and decide if you want to do more or not. So you are always planning for a couple of weeks at a time. To plan a larger cycle, you estimate a series of short implementation cycles.

Many people ask me about using EVM (Earned Value Management) for Agile projects. Of course you can do it, but the information is not very meaningful for Agile because it measures the wrong thing. Remember that in Waterfall our focus is on delivering a project on time and budget (EVM measures this). But in Agile our focus is on delivering the right product to end users (EVM does not measure this). Remember also that delivering a project on time and budget is not a predictor of delivering the right product. EVM does not provide the information an Agile team needs.

Rather than thinking of weeks or months, a better approach is to base Agile estimates on work packages. Because each work package is relatively small and nearly independent, this gives you an easy and fairly accurate way to determine what a specified deliverable will cost. When you plan upcoming work, you pick the work packages you want implemented. Add up their estimated duration and cost and you have the estimates for a larger effort.

Basing Agile metrics on work packages tells you not only if the project is on time and budget, but they also tell if you have working software and whether or not that software is correct. Our metrics around work packages are these: is this work package complete or not (100% or zero), and is the work package accepted by the user or user representative. When work packages are not complete or accepted, you can track how much work is slipping to detect very early if the team is getting into trouble or you are confident they will complete what they said on time.

Another thing we want to measure is the team. Do they deliver as promised? Is this improving or not? Is the pace of their work varying by more than 10% per implementation cycle? If you measure the percent of work completed and the percent of money spent, are those percentages approximately equal?

We also want to assess the value or importance of each work package. Then you can determine the percent of value that has been implemented. How does that number compare to percent of money and time? Even more interesting, what is the overall trend for this team? Are they trending better or worse? If you have quality standards in place, then you can also measure the quality of the product delivered, and the trend over time to see if the quality is improving or worsening.

It is important to measure by percentage so you can compare one team to another, even though the teams may be doing very different work. It is also important to measure trends to see if the situation is improving or getting worse. A team may appear to be doing fine today, but their overall trend is that they are getting into trouble. Another team may appear to be in trouble, but their overall trend is that they are progressing well toward completion. By measuring trends, you can be proactive when managing projects, programs, releases, or portfolios instead of reacting after there is already a problem.

Because we want to deliver the right product at the right time for the right ROI, we also need to evaluate the success of the product after delivery. We need to determine if the users think this is the right product and we need to measure the actual ROI. Very few large companies are doing this. This is largely due to work being organized as projects. Once the project is over, there is no one available to do the work of finding out if customers are satisfied or if we actually achieved the estimated return on investment. Companies that have an Asset Steward type role (such as a Product Manager) have someone who is (or can be) responsible for collecting this kind of information and using it to plan future work.

Corporate Structures that Make Agile Metrics Very Difficult or Expensive

Most of what you see today in very large companies is that a project is created with a certain amount of money and a deadline associated with it. Then a detailed project plan is made showing all the things to be done from start to finish with estimates of hours/money for each segment of the plan. As the project goes along, the project manager reports how much has been done. This is all very easy to implement and consume. Reports tend to show red, yellow, green flags for status to say a project is in trouble, may need help, or is going well.

The Agile metrics mean more work for managers because they require the managers to evaluate the data they are seeing, not just look for red, yellow, or green indicators based on time and money. Someone has to go look at the working product and evaluate if it is acceptable or not. The manager has to deal with the team being unhappy at only reporting all or nothing completion status. The team has to create good work packages, estimate them, and report against them, which is new. Managers have to learn to use trending data, and understand the relationships between percentage work complete, percentage budget spent, and percentage value implemented.

This can all be automated and training can be provided. But I have encountered over and over strong resistance to using anything but EVM metrics. I am given two reasons most often. The first is that management wants all projects, Agile or not, to use the same metrics and be on the same report. The second reason is that many different kinds of managers I have showed Agile metrics to claimed that they understood the metrics just fine but were sure their peers would not.

A final difficulty I have found is tool support for Agile metrics. Several of the most common tool suites used in large companies for tracking projects, programs, and portfolios, even those that claim they support Agile, actually do not allow the collection or reporting of Agile metrics. They would have to be customized to support it or a different tool suite put in place. People I know successfully using Agile metrics started with spreadsheets, and when they discovered the usefulness, shared the knowledge with others until enough people were using these metrics that the company decided to create the automation for them.

Corporate Structures that Make Agile Metrics Easier

Companies that use Agile metrics successfully focus on reporting status based on work packages. When that is done, it does not matter if the work package is being implemented as a standalone effort (such as fixing a critical defect), or if it is part of a project, program, or product release. Another change is to use metrics based on percentages rather than metrics based on raw numbers. This allows for the same metrics, the same reporting, for radically different kinds of work. When management understands the use of trending data rather than point data, then Agile metrics are easy to implement.

A number of companies have implemented their own internal tools for reporting up through the management chain. These internal tools support the collection of work package level information, the calculation of percentages based on a goal (such as project end or release date), and merging data using company specific algorithms into red, yellow, green flags with trending indicators. The tool allows managers to treat yellow trending green differently than yellow trending red, so they can focus their attention on the teams most likely to be having problems. These companies have hands on managers who really pay attention to what their people are doing.

The Surprising Thing That Makes Agile Metrics Really Difficult

The biggest reason companies do not want Agile metrics is that above the level of project manager everyone wants there to be nothing but green on the status report. With this kind of reward in place, project managers play games with the data to ensure that no matter what is going on, unless there is a complete disaster, everything is always reported green. Project managers and implementation teams tend to be optimistic folk. Sure we are having some problems, but we'll get it fixed and get caught up, so don't bother anyone above us with any information other than we are doing fine. If we report anything else, we just get in trouble which is bad for our careers.

Expecting everything to be green all the time is unrealistic and just hides real problems. The project team hopes the issues will not be discovered until after they are finished, so it becomes someone else's problem. The project team does not get in trouble (they have long been disbanded when it is found) and the operations teams who get to fix it are not blamed for it because they did not develop the solution to begin with. It appears everyone wins in this situation. Management can say we are the best organization in the world because everything is perfect all the time, and the implementation teams can say we have always been successful, which looks really good on a resume.

But the cost is very large to the company. The later the problems are fixed, the more expensive they are, by a dramatically large amount. They are expensive because something that could have been easily fixed early on is hidden until the problem is really big. When I say really large, the difference is it costs X if fixed immediately and 1000X if it is fixed after the asset is in production.

Rewarding for honesty and the occasional failure is a completely different mindset that yields much greater overall cost reduction and increase in efficiency. I know of one company that says if you have had no failures in the past year, you are not doing your job effectively. Of course a person cannot constantly fail but nor can someone constantly succeed. Finding the right balance brings overall the lowest cost, highest quality, and allows for innovation and great breakthroughs.

Thomas Edison, one of our world's greatest inventors, thought there was no such thing as failure. He just learned how not to do something, and those experiences led to the correct solution. Toyota set up an automated, highly efficient factory to build cars. The robots do the job correctly every time. But they do not innovate. Failure requires us to find a solution, which leads to innovation. If you do not allow failure, you do not allow innovation. If you have a culture of hiding information, you will not be able to find and fix inefficiencies nor to detect when you are spending far more than you need to.

Chapter 17

Agile Controls for Risk

C ontrols, by definition, are processes and procedures. Specifically controls are not documents. If we are to consider what an Agile control is, we have to look at the various Agile practices. There are many, many controls in Agile due to the way the implementation team interacts with each other, the customer, and the user. In this section, I will cover a small number of the most fundamental Agile controls. These mitigate the risk of controlling for the wrong thing, thus causing some risk to not be mitigated.

Fundamentally the business risks we need to control for are wrong solution, delivered at the wrong time, poor ROI, and poor quality (which can include lack of adherence to regulatory requirements). Any one of these can be a significant negative impact on the profitability of the company. It is much worse in combination. I think Next Computer was a great example – the initial product was shipped at the wrong time (I could argue either too early or too late), at too high of a price (much more expensive than the PC's buyers were comparing it to), with features that most corporate buyers did not see the need for. The company failed.

Agile controls for these risks differently than Waterfall. The most important Agile controls are:

1. Demonstrate a working solution every delivery cycle (increment, sprint) to real users and respond to their feedback. This controls for the risks of wrong solution, wrong time, and poor quality.
2. Asset Steward (business) decides when to release the solution, not the implementation team. Even more ideally, the users de-

cide when the solution will be released. This controls for the risk of wrong time.

3. Deliver the highest value work first, where highest value is determined by the Asset Steward (business) and the users. This controls for the risks of poor ROI and wrong solution.
4. Validation (testing, audit, review) is an integral part of implementation, not a separate stage. This controls for the risk of poor quality.

The practice that enables the others is for the Asset Steward (business) to maintain a prioritized queue of relatively small, nearly independent, well-defined work packages (the first of the Big Three Management practices). I consider this to be the most fundamental control. I have seen this fundamental control used in such diverse settings as hospitals, software development, robot development, wedding planning, and musical theater production for just a few examples.

These Agile controls are very different from Waterfall controls that are used to control for success or failure of the project. The Agile controls are for the risk of the success or failure of the solution with the users which is far more important to the long term health of your company. Project success in no way predicts the success of the solution for the users.

Corporate Structures that Make Agile Controls Very Difficult or Expensive

In many large companies, some technical part of the company (IT, Operations, Software Delivery) is used to making all the decisions about the asset. The expectation is that business will write the requirements and then not engage with the implementation team again until the end of the project. Since the Agile controls require the participation of the business or are actively performed by the business, this is a big change for everyone.

When adopting Agile, the most common question I am asked by the business is "How much more time will my people have to put into this compared to Waterfall?" Most of the time, the business does not want to be more involved because it does take more of their time and they do not see the value for themselves. Those who have really tried Agile invariably love the control it gives the business over the assets they manage.

Many on the business side resist Agile because they do not want the responsibility for making decisions about their assets. What if they are wrong! This is where a culture that punishes failure makes it difficult to impossible to adopt Agile controls.

Many large companies have a separate QA department responsible for validation and testing of assets as well as performing traditional Quality Assurance. The QA group expects to receive the asset at a defined point in time when they will do all the testing and validation. Their processes and procedures are not set up to support embedding testers into the implementation team. The testers do not know how to work side by side with implementers, and the implementers do not know how to chunk their work to make this possible. When I work with implementation teams on the validation control the most common reaction is "We cannot chunk our work in small pieces to enable testing to begin earlier. It has to be all done and then handed off." This is because they do not know how. It can absolutely be done for every kind of work I have seen in my lengthy and varied career.

Sometimes your security, legal, or corporate communications groups may prevent you from demonstrating working software to real users. There may be concerns about bringing outsiders onsite, competitors finding out about the asset before we are ready to release it, liability, damage to reputation, or implied contracts. The most effective demonstrations of progress are in front of different users/user groups each time so that you get a representative sample overall. This may be MUCH harder to do than getting permission for a small number of well-vetted users to be allowed to see the asset early.

Corporate Structures that Make Agile Controls Easier

Companies with a strong Asset Stewardship discipline (often found in Product Managers in Marketing) more easily adopt these Agile controls. Asset Stewards in general are very much in tune with the market and users, and as a result expect to be much more involved in the development of the asset. Asset Stewardship is different from Project Management, Program Management, and Portfolio Management. Asset Stewardship is somewhat broader than the job done by most Product Managers.

Asset Stewardship activities are not explored in Agile methodologies, which tend to focus on the implementation team almost exclusively. Some do describe aspects of Program and Portfolio Management. But Asset Stewardship is extremely important for companies that wish to be Agile in their markets.

Asset Stewards are responsible for the value of the asset to the company over a very long time, therefore they are very interested in keeping quality high. A quality asset has the longest useful lifetime for the lowest lifetime cost of ownership. Thus a quality asset is of the highest overall value to the company.

An Asset Steward will generally be happy to review the working solution at the end of each delivery cycle (sprint, increment). This gives the Asset Steward more information to make decisions about the asset.

In addition to Asset Stewardship, early and frequent testing is an important control. This is best done at the same time as the solution is being implemented, not just at the end. Companies with fewer specialties tend to have an easier time integrating validation with implementation. Developers are used to doing at least some of their own testing as they implement the solution, with independent testers more involved when the work of many people is put together and tests are run on the end-to-end solution.

The Surprising Thing That Makes Agile Controls Really Difficult

Audit processes in most large companies are based around verifying that some set of documents has been completed. These audits tend to be performed once after a project has completed. The risk and control officers have a sense of safety when the documents are in place and are extremely uncomfortable with projects that do not have documents. Processes are transient things; documents live on and can be referenced in case of outside audit or lawsuit. They often feel that using processes for risk mitigation (instead of documents)means there is no control.

If your company moves away from projects to continuous streams of work, this also causes a problem for the auditors. If there is no project to end, when do they audit? The typical solution to this is to audit whenever there is a formal release to production. If releases to production are on short schedules, such as daily, weekly, or monthly, this is undoubtedly much too often for auditors to keep up, and so a different audit point must be chosen.

In Agile we focus on the practices as controls, but there can still be documentation created that indicates the practices themselves were audited. In one Fortune 50 company I know, observation of the practices was used as an audit procedure, with the auditor filing a report of their findings. The report documented that the practices had been done, any errors in performing the practices, and noted when the practices were not done. This approach provided a trail that showed the controls were in place and being audited.

Auditing processes and practices is much more time consuming than verifying that the required documentation is in place. An effective approach I have seen used is to ask Project Managers to audit implementation teams they are not otherwise involved with and prepare the reports. Then the auditors can verify that the audit reports have been completed. This may not be sufficient in a heavily regulated environment where there may be fear of collusion among the Project Managers to give each other good audits. It is also still time consuming but your company probably has far more Project Managers than you do Auditors so the work load is spread out.

Chapter 18

Organize Work Around Capital Assets

A project is a way to structure and account for work. When there is a problem identified, a project may be proposed to fix the problem. The solution that the project will implement is limited by time and money. A program is a very large project or a group of related projects. The lifetime of a project is typically measured in months, the lifetime of a program is typically 3 years or less. A Project or Program Manager is only responsible for the duration of the project (or program).

A capital asset is something that your company manages over the long term. An Asset Steward is someone responsible for the long term stewardship of a capital asset. Capital assets are things your company purchases as well as products your company produces for sale. The lifetime of a capital asset is typically 5 years and more. Products that your company sells may have a lifetime in decades. Some companies have products they have been selling for more than 100 years.

The value of managing an asset with a long term view in mind is that you reduce the lifetime cost of ownership and increase the usable lifetime of the asset. Having someone responsible for the asset and knowing its market allows the company to quickly respond to market changes.

All work done on a capital asset should be viewed as part of an overall vision. Instead of individual projects to fix or add features, all work on the asset is part of a planned continuum. When a capital asset needs some work - creating a new feature, fixing a defect, or installing an update - that work should be considered as part of the lifetime maintenance of the asset, and not as individual point solutions.

Projects are good in many circumstances, but they have been misused to manage every kind of work. In some cases, decisions made in the short term focus of a project may be detrimental to the long term maintenance of the asset. Some will say they have been successfully managing assets using projects for a long time. But when you look at the total cost of ownership of the asset over decades, managing the work as projects with their short term focus almost always leads to significant cost in the long term that is not incurred when the asset is managed as a long term commitment.

The difference is apparent when you consider what is being managed. With a project focus, a Project Manager is managing the project. The project is an entity that is being managed and the Project Manager is rewarded for successfully delivering the project. With an asset focus, the Asset Steward is managing the asset itself. The asset is the entity that is being managed and the Asset Steward is rewarded for good financial management of the asset over the long term.

A project is a perfect choice for efforts that are "one and done". They typically are done to manage work around 3rd party products, such as upgrading everyone to Windows 7, or one time efforts such as moving data from an old database into a new database.

Managing assets as an ongoing series of releases is the best choice for something your company is responsible for maintaining over many, many years. Proprietary systems you have developed, internally developed training, the products and services you sell should all be managed with a long term view in mind. You should also take a long term ownership view of strategic areas of your company, such as supply chain, even when all the supporting software is provided by 3rd parties.

When work is managed as projects, it is hard to respond to changes in the market or user expectations. This is because the Project Manager is not responsible for addressing those changes. The Project Manager is responsible for delivering the scope on time and on budget and is typically accountable to portfolio managers.

When an asset view is taken, there is a long term vision for the asset. Because someone is responsible for the asset, that person can quickly make decisions that are consistent with the long term view but also address sudden changes in the market. The Asset Steward is responsible for the asset's return on investment over the long term and is typically accountable to business line management.

Funding is different in each case as well. Each project is individually funded and accounted for. A capital asset typically has a yearly budget which is the responsibility of the Asset Steward to spend wisely to increase profitability and keep overall costs low.

It is not just management that has a different focus when considering projects versus assets. With a project focus, the implementation team members are brought together at the start of the project, then disbanded at the end. An individual is moved around from project to project and often does not get to know much about any one asset. Fixing any problems that are discovered becomes someone else's problem in the push to deliver on time. With an asset focus, a team of implementers is kept together as an asset team. They do all the work on the asset and get to know it very well. It is in their best interests to fix problems as they find them.

Corporate Structures that Make Capital Asset Focus Very Difficult or Expensive

If you company has no Asset Stewards, then you will not have people who know how to manage assets. Asset Stewards are trained in very different skills and techniques than Project Managers. You cannot just change the title of a Project Manager to Asset Steward and expect that person to succeed. Companies that require their managers to have PMP certification (Project Management Professional) have a very difficult time changing to a focus on assets because all their people are trained to manage projects not assets.

When your company rewards people for short term successes, when people are rewarded for doing it fast instead of doing it right, then decisions will be made that are detrimental to the long term health of the asset. No one thinks of it that way, but the end result of short term thinking is high technical debt and a greatly increased total cost of ownership over the lifetime of the asset.

In an environment of fear of failure no one wants to be responsible or accountable for decisions. This leads to a situation where too many people are responsible for results. I know of one Fortune 200 company that has 4 different people with manager in their title who are responsible for delivering a project on time and on budget (each reporting to a different chain of command), and 3-5 people responsible for defining the vision for each asset. There was no clear guidance on anything with all those competing concerns. In this kind of environment it is not at all unusual for significant asset decisions to be made by junior programmers because they have to code something in order to deliver the project and no one is providing direction. And that junior programmer is safe because if anything goes wrong "She is new, she did not know better".

With software assets, the creation of separate development, devOps, and operations departments makes asset focus very difficult or expensive. This is another example of making a lot of people responsible for something (in this case software) so no one is responsible. The development group does not feel responsible for the maintainability of the code because they will not be responsible for maintaining it. In the end the operations group has to deal with messy code that is expensive to maintain, but since their job is to respond to critical problems, they do not feel responsible for fixing the long term problem. Messy software is expensive to maintain and the problem only gets worse over time.

People should work on one asset long enough that they get to know the asset and feel responsible for it. Instead of creating projects, create asset implementation and support teams that stay together over many years. Rotate some percentage of people each year between assets to broaden their experience, but keep asset teams themselves stable.

Corporate Structures that Make Capital Asset Focus Easier

Companies that can easily focus on assets have a strong Asset Stewardship discipline with defined decision points appropriate to that discipline. For example, given what is currently in production, what has been implemented since the last release, user feedback at the demonstrations since the last release, the measured ROI to date, what the competitors are doing, and any changes or disruptive technologies that have occurred in our market:

- Should we release what is currently implemented at this time, at another time, or never?
- Should we continue doing more work on this asset in the near future or is it good enough at this time?
- Should we continue to invest in this asset at all or is it time to stop investing?
- Does stop investing mean end this asset completely, replace the asset with something new, continue to support what is currently in production but do no new development, sell the asset to someone other company to maintain until there are no more users, or some other decision?

For fast-changing assets, this review may be a weekly, bi-weekly, or monthly consideration. For medium-changing assets, this may be quarterly or 1/2 year. For slow-changing assets, yearly may be sufficient. This kind of decision making by an Asset Steward who is responsible for the long term success of the asset provides the environment for agile responses to changes in the market or disruptive technologies.

While rewarding Asset Stewards for the asset's success, you also have to reward them for recognizing decline and managing that decline in a way of most benefit to the company and the customers. Part of Kodak's difficulties in the early 2000's was not addressing the declining film market soon enough. Part of Fuji's success was accepting the declining market for film and finding new products to produce and sell. Fuji remained very profitable even as film products accounted for less and less of their sales.

When executive management is rewarded for looking for 3-5 year gains, it is easier to make changes in the company to support long term asset focus. There is executive awareness of the total lifetime cost of ownership of an asset and a corporate goal to keep that as low as possible. Instead of just rewarding people for short term success, people are rewarded for balancing short-term and long-term gains and costs.

On the implementation side, asset implementation teams stay together and own everything about implementing and maintaining the asset. There is no handoff of the asset to a separate maintenance or operations team.

The Surprising Thing That Makes Capital Asset Focus Really Difficult

When the accounting systems, reports, and metrics are designed around projects, it may be extremely difficult to move to an asset focus. These systems can handle programs because programs are treated as really big projects, but capital asset focus leads to different accounting structures, different reporting, and different metrics. Assets do not end for decades, there is nothing to close out. We report on the success of the asset in the marketplace instead of the reporting on the schedule and budget of a project.

I am often told "We cannot change our accounting. Changing it is too hard, too expensive, or too time consuming. And while I understand your approach to asset accounting, my peers are not as smart and will not be able to do this."

Companies also tell me they cannot change reporting or metrics because then they cannot compare past performance to current and future performance. Or they will be unable to compare themselves to competitors in the market.

All of this is resolvable, but do you have the political capital to institute widespread changes in accounting, reporting, and metrics? Yes we can track expensed versus capitalized labor in an asset model. Each point in time that a new version of an asset is available to users (a release point) is when you can capitalize. And while many in the Agile community push for releases as short as every 2 weeks, there is no particular reason to do that for most of the capital assets maintained by large corporations. You can balance expenses and capitalization even without projects.

Chapter 19

Minimum Viable Product (MVP)

The idea of Minimum Viable Product (MVP) was popularized by the Lean Startup movement, though it has its roots in engineering practices going back to the Romans. The basic idea is to do a little, then test to see if you are on the right track. If not, try again with a different approach. If it is good, add a bit more. Obviously you would not do this with a large physical object like a bridge, but you would do this with a model of a bridge before investing in the complete structure. This is a powerful mitigation strategy for the risk of doing the wrong thing or creating the wrong product.

MVP is a way to test out ideas in the least expensive way before making a large investment. Sometimes the result of MVP is to cancel the whole effort, sometimes it is to release less than you anticipated, sometimes it is to release something different than what you planned. This is a very powerful technique to get the right product to market for less risk and lower cost than other approaches.

How it works in modern corporations is that based on market research you create mockups, prototypes, or full implementations of a very small amount of functionality. This should be the minimum thing you can think of that would provide some value to end users. Then you get your mockups, prototypes, or small product in front of real users and let them play with it.

The optimum way to do this is observe the users interacting with your product in their environment. Next best is to invite users to your site to interact with your product and observe what they do. If you are able to release an actual implementation to the market or a select group of users, then you have to be sure to provide a mechanism for feedback and you have to monitor social media sites to see what people are saying about the product. MVP is typically easiest to do when you are working with internal users.

How you make this feedback from users happen will be different at different stages of the product lifecycle. If it is a new product, then you will likely want more control over the process to limit how much information gets out before you are ready. If it is a new feature you want to test on an existing product, you might just release it to everyone and see what happens. Alpha and Beta releases are traditional ways to get feedback from a limited number of users before you are ready to let everyone have the new product or feature.

The important thing about releasing an MVP is to quickly act on the feedback you receive from the users. It is not so bad if what the users want are some adjustments, but are you prepared for complete rejection of your great new idea? It can happen. The good news is you limited your investment to a small piece when you found out that it was the wrong approach. You might decide to stop development completely or to try something new.

If feedback is negative, you need a good way to pull the new product or new feature without causing problems with existing products. If you released the new product or feature broadly, you may have to do this very quickly to avoid possible damage to your company reputation or brand. If Facebook puts out a feature that people start commenting negatively on, it could be gone within hours.

Once you have released the MVP and found it was the right thing to do, you can continue building on that success with additional features. Each time you release just enough to provide value and get feedback from your users.

Corporate Structures that Make MVP Very Difficult or Expensive

If you do not have someone who can quickly make decisions based on the feedback from users about the product, then you get no value from MVP. Someone has to review the feedback and make a decision or there was no point to the exercise.

If you do not have a way to get feedback from real users to decision makers, then you lose most of the advantage of releasing a small amount at a time. The decision makers get to see it at demonstrations (assuming you are regularly demonstrating a working solution) and they can provide feedback based on their own knowledge. But this does not really replace feedback from actual users.

Sometimes feedback is collected but it is filtered through layers of management who put their own best spin on the information before the information is given to the decision maker. Now the decision maker does not really know what the users want but rather the interpretation of various managers of what the users want. I know of quite a number of cases where the users did not want a product but by the time various managers had "cleaned up" the data, it appeared to the decision makers that the users were delighted by the product.

You cannot really support MVP if you do not have the infrastructure to support short releases and fast rollbacks when something goes wrong. The point of MVP is to get feedback as inexpensively as possible, so if you have to do a lot of manual work, the cost may overcome the benefit.

MVP may not work for physical products because of the high cost of production. There are still ways around it, such as making a limited prototype to show at an industry trade show to get feedback, but it is more of a challenge. 3-d printers are making it easier to test out ideas for some physical products at fairly low cost. This makes MVP becomes more feasible for physical products than ever before.

If your customer base is disengaged or disinterested you will not receive very much feedback, if any at all. If this is the situation, you likely have a much larger issue. It is possible if you can get anyone to provide feedback, and demonstrate a response to that feedback, this could be a way to gradually get your customers more interested (and likely improve your market share).

In an environment where failure is punished, it may be too risky to try an MVP approach. What if you discover the users hate your new product or new features? If we keep developing until we have a lot to release, there is bound to be something the users like, so we can declare victory. I think it is actually good to find out early that there are problems before you spend a lot of money, but the idea of failing fast so you can succeed sooner is not always welcome.

In some companies, there is so much concern about the competition finding out what you are doing that you are not allowed to take a test and learn approach. Sometimes Legal or Corporate Communications, in their concern about company reputation or fear of lawsuits, may block this approach.

If your work is organized as well-defined projects, MVP is much harder. This is because the purpose of MVP is test and learn, so we cannot define the results up front. In fact, we want to be able to change course based on user feedback. In a project-focused company, this involves a change process which can be very lengthy. One team I know that was attempting MVP in a project based environment ran out of work to do while waiting on a change request to be approved, because any additional work depended on the response to the change request. They sat for 4 weeks waiting for an executive decision (and yes, the executive was told everyone was waiting on him). The executive did not mind paying for people to not work because he wanted to spend all his budget so he could ask for more. This is not an environment where MVP works.

Corporate Structures that Make MVP Easier

Working with an MVP is much easier when you have an actual Asset

Steward responsible for the performance of the product. Such a person will be interested in any approach that will get them closer to the real users and their needs. When we meet the user's needs, we make more sales.

If you have an active, engaged customer base, perhaps through a company blog, a Facebook page, or a similar social media presence, then you have the people you need to provide you real feedback on your products. Most very large companies have hired people to monitor social media to find out what their customers really think.

If the budget for work is tied to a product rather than to specific projects, this makes it easier to do MVP. The reason is that if budget is tied to a project, and you cancel the project because you determine it was the wrong thing to do, in order to spend the money saved on something else someone has to go through the whole project proposal process (which in big companies is often a long painful process). If the product is funded for the year, and you cancel some bit of work because the users told you they did not want it, you just start your implementation team working on the next most important thing.

When it is easy for decision makers to get the real feedback from users, MVP is much easier. A number of companies set up observation rooms where a user is invited to see and interact with the MVP, often guided by a User Experience (UX) expert. A mirrored wall allows others to watch and listen. The important thing is that the actual decision makers are observing. It is a powerful experience for executives to watch real users interact with their product.

A product focused company, or one that promotes innovation, is a natural fit for an MVP approach.

The Surprising Thing That Makes MVP Really Difficult

The funding game throughout a large percentage of the Fortune 500 works essentially like this: Your budget for next year is usually what you spent last year with maybe a percentage increase. This motivates executives in the various areas to encourage their people to spend all of their budget before the end of the year, and even ask for more. If we do not spend all our money this year, then the portfolio team will decide we don't need so much, and so will reduce our budget next year and give the money to someone else.

Some signs that this might be the case at your company include things such as large purchases of office supplies or hardware in December. Or an effort becomes critical in early November requiring us to bring in a bunch of contractors for November – December. I have done quite a bit of corporate training in December when companies are looking for ways to spend money and the pace of work is slower.

Often executives make their own lives easier by requiring every Project Manager to bring in the project on budget. The Project Manager may actually get in trouble for saving money because now the executive (who thought his budget was all accounted for) has to find someplace to spend that money or risk losing it the next year. Sometimes a Project Manager is rewarded for going just a little over budget (not a lot because that is a problem). The small amounts over budget per project can add up to a significant increase in what that department needs for the next year.

If this is the process in your company, then MVP is a difficult sell. If the users always love what you put in front of them, or like it well enough that a few adjustments take care of any issues, there is less of an issue. But when you reach a point where the users say they do not want any more at this time, or they reject a product or feature set, suddenly you have nothing more to spend money on. I know teams who implement features the users don't want so they can spend all their money.

The idea of MVP is not at issue. It is the consequences of MVP that are at odds with how things are supposed to work. If using MVP means you are saving money while delighting the customers (a typical result), then you will have to be on top of finding ways to spend more money in an environment when you have to spend it all every year.

This kind of funding approach is typically accompanied by an environment where the bigger your budget the more power you have. Thus people are rewarded for needing a bigger and bigger budget every year. Those who really try to be the most efficient, and therefore actually bring the company more gain, often must give up any ideas of positions of power within the company.

It can get pretty ridiculous. I had one project manager come to me nearly in tears because she was so frustrated. Her boss said to get promoted she had to manage $5 million in projects in a year. It did not matter if it was one $5 million project or five $1 million projects, it was the total that mattered. Now clearly managing one $5 million project is a bigger, more responsible position, but she could devote all her time to it. Instead she was going crazy trying to manage 5 projects at once, and none were getting the time they needed from her. That is the kind of behavior you get when rewarding based on size of budget rather than results.

Chapter 20

Continuous Delivery

C ontinuous delivery allows a company to be extremely agile in responding to changes in the market. This is what allows companies such as Google, Facebook, and Amazon to release product very quickly. If you have products in fast changing markets, continuous delivery is what will let you keep up with or surpass the competition.

Continuous delivery means the implementation team keeps the product in a state where it is always ready to release. This includes making sure the product meets all quality standards. Every change is releasable. If the teams are good at chunking their work into small bits, you may have releasable product at least every day, and sometimes multiple times a day. At any time a decision maker can, in some sense, just push a button and the product is almost instantly available to the users.

Continuous deployment takes continuous delivery one step further and actually pushes the changes to users every time a change is made. For many products, this is not necessary, may be overwhelming to end users, and may have a negative impact on the financial status of the company because everything now becomes an expense.

Continuous delivery requires large amounts of automation and infrastructure to support it. Google has a whole team that they call the Engineering Productivity team whose job it is to make continuous delivery possible. Before deciding that you want to implement continuous delivery, consider the gain you will get from it and consider the cost. The cost will be setting up the infrastructure and automation, staffing the support team (whatever you call them), and the cost of making the change.

It is very likely that some of your products will benefit a lot more from continuous delivery than others. It may be so costly to make continuous delivery possible for some of your products that it is not worth implementing continuous delivery for those products.

Corporate Structures that Make Continuous Delivery Very Difficult or Expensive

Continuous delivery is not possible when your products are tightly tied together. An indicator that this might be a problem is that product releases have to be coordinated with each other. You may find there is a long period (I have seen anywhere from 2-6 weeks in recent years) before the release date that is required to integrate and test across product lines. Another indicator of this problem is that changes to one product impact other products. When you see these issues, in order to make continuous delivery possible, the products have to be re-architected to remove dependencies, which could be a multi-year effort.

It surprises me how much testing is still manual. Manual testing means a person tests the product. Automated testing means a machine and software are used to test the product. The ability to automate testing (especially of software) has been around for at least 20 years. The tools and techniques are well known. Manual testing is extremely slow compared to automated testing. Because it is so time consuming, teams only want to test once at the end of a project and not test throughout. If they test something earlier and that thing then changes, then that test has to be repeated. With automation, testing can be done continuously because it is cheap and easy. If your teams are still doing mostly manual testing, continuous delivery will be very expensive and infeasible.

Another barrier to continuous delivery is a lot of manual intervention to move the product from implementation, through integration, testing, and finally deployment. I have seen a process in a number of companies where a person was notified that software was ready to integrate, then that person physically copied files from one computer to another where the integration would occur. And this process was repeated for each stage of the deployment process. One Fortune 200 company I know in the past required a manager signoff each time the product moved. You are not likely to have releasable product daily if 3-6 managers have to approve the movement of the product from stage to stage of the release process.

If your projects end with a hardening phase of several weeks to make the product actually ready for release, you are not able to do continuous delivery. Continuous delivery implies that every change leaves the product in a releasable state. A hardening phase is where many changes are put together for final testing and fixing before release. This is not continuous delivery.

If you company has silos of implementers, testers, release engineers, and maintenance engineers then continuous delivery is very difficult due to the need for all these people to coordinate their work. With many people involved, the work tends to go back and forth as issues are resolved. Someone implements part of the solution, someone else tests it and finds a problem, it goes back to the implementer (who is probably already working on something else), sometime later a fix is made, it goes back to a tester, who may then approve it to go to the build engineer, who may find a problem in integration and return it to the implementer and so on through the whole process. The work goes much faster when implementers are also expected to test.

Corporate Structures that Make Continuous Delivery Easier

Companies that are able to do continuous delivery have products that are designed to be independent of each other. There are well-defined interfaces to shared resources and well-defined protocols for changing shared resources. Product teams are independent of each other and therefore can release their products independently of each other. There is no multi-week effort to integrate all the products before they can be released all together because there is no need to release them all together.

Companies with continuous delivery have an infrastructure to support an automated deployment pipeline including continuous integration and build servers, automated test suites at all levels from unit test to system and integration test, and automated moves from development to test to production. Often there is a team whose job it is to make everyone else more effective and efficient by creating and supporting infrastructure, building tools, building frameworks, and creating the broad scale tests that run automatically over large amounts of the product.

When I started my career as a programmer, I was expected to write software, test the software, perform first stage integration, and run more tests on the integrated code. Testing was an integral part of implementation, not a separate activity. Today, companies who are doing continuous delivery have returned to the practice of implementers also testing their work. Testing by a separate organization happens when the work of many implementers is put together, and not before then.

Companies that require user acceptance testing can still do continuous delivery when the user is closely involved with the implementation team. I know several teams in a multi-billion dollar company who show every change to their users as soon as possible after the change is complete. Generally this means they meet with the users daily, though sometimes they get together two or three times a day. They can do this because they are working with internal users. They are able to do continuous delivery because the acceptance testing is an integral part of implementation, not something tacked on the end.

Companies doing continuous delivery make the teams responsible and accountable for their work, rather than asking for a manager sign off on the work. These teams also divide their work into very small pieces so any particular change is low risk and can be easily rolled back.

The Surprising Thing That Makes Continuous Delivery Really Difficult

Many very large companies are turning to coordinated releases across their product lines to solve a variety of quality problems in released products. It is seen as a solution, when in fact it merely hides the root causes of the quality problems, allowing them to continue and potentially making matters worse over time. Companies that require coordinated releases are not able to do continuous delivery.

One of the most common reasons that companies get to a position to require coordinated releases is organizing all work into projects and measuring success by the project completed on time and on budget. This combined with a push for ever shorter time to market and a desire to cut costs by hiring fewer (and typically more junior) implementers leads to teams abandoning the practices that make the product easy to maintain. They do not have the time to make the product maintainable and at the same time meet ever shorter deadlines with fewer people.

When a product is easy to maintain, work on that product can be divided into small pieces that are quick to implement. Also, that product will have extensive suites of automated tests, many of which are built into the product itself, and others are supported by frameworks. The writing of the automated tests and the creation of frameworks and test harnesses takes time, but the time invested today pays dividends in the future with reduced cost of maintenance and the ability to deliver continuously.

Project managers do not want to invest in that time today because you are rewarding them for completing the project on time and on budget, not rewarding them for making the job of maintaining and enhancing that product easier in the future. Focusing on short term deadlines makes continuous delivery really difficult.

Section Five

Structuring a Naturally Agile Company

We keep moving forward, opening new doors, and doing new things, because we're curious and curiosity keeps leading us down new paths.

- Walt Disney

An Introduction to the Practices

I have had the great fortune of working for companies that were structured in such a way that working in an Agile manner was not only easy, it was the obvious way to work. In this section, I will outline this natural Agile structure. The further your company is from this, the harder it will be to implement Agile practices.

There are a couple of reasons why structuring your company for Agile will benefit you. One reason this natural Agile structure is good is that it maximizes the throughput of your production system. Another is that a natural Agile structure makes it easy to make change when it is needed.

Many decades of manufacturing show that optimizing for an individual (whether person, process, or machine) does not give you the greatest efficiency. Optimizing for throughput of the whole system, from request to fulfillment of the request, gives you the most efficiency, which balances time to market with cost.

Traditional company structures around silos of specialists look good on paper. It appears you have removed waste by making each person as optimized as possible. It is also believed to be a good way to reduce the amount of staff required. In practice, this ends up creating organizations full of people who cannot keep up with the load. When others request their services, the requests take a long time to fill, thus creating blockages in the process. In an effort to completely optimize individuals, we have created a lot of wasted time in the system overall.

As an individual, full optimization is exhausting. The person is working full out all day every day without mental down time. Many people think they are working that way when independent observation proves that most people actually work on task maybe half the time.

I have been in companies where they succeeded in reaching full optimization goals for their employees in some departments. Those departments had by far the highest turnover of any part of the company to the point where it was a huge problem for them. People left because they were exhausted.

Optimizing throughput leads to a very different kind of company structure which I outline in this section. While each individual person may not be fully optimized all the time, the end-to-end flow is faster and more efficient without blockages creating wasted time and delay. Your customers do not care if each of your employees is fully optimized. Your customers care if you satisfy their needs in a timely manner.

An Agile structure also helps you change course quickly. By letting people close to the work make decisions, keeping delivery cycles short, getting frequent feedback, and having processes in place to quickly respond to that feedback, you are in a position to be able to pivot in response to changing conditions.

Along with Agile structures it is important to develop throughout your organization a mental mindset of flexibility and of not having to be right all the time. People who have to be right all the time are resistant to change, even when change is what the company needs. When people are punished for failure, they will not take the risk of speaking up when something is going wrong. These are reasons why developing the right mindset is also critically important.

The final chapters examine how an Agile company structures the workforce, the work, and the infrastructure.

Chapter 21

Structure the Workforce for Agile

W hen considering the optimal environment for Agile, you want to consider how you structure the workforce to best support Agile. You have to consider the need to keep whole teams together, but also the need to develop specialized knowledge. How will you help people develop in their careers in a way that balances the company need for specialists and generalists? How can you support the people who want to work from home? These are the topics we consider in this chapter:

1. Organize tribes around capital assets and service offerings
2. Create guilds for specialities
3. Organize careers around goals
4. How to incorporate remote workers

Organize communities around capital assets and service offerings

There are a number of reasons for organizing your work force in this manner. By putting everyone who does work on a capital asset or service offering together, you build a lot of expert knowledge within the community. As individuals develop deep domain knowledge, it becomes possible for them to try different kinds of work within the community, thus encouraging generalists to develop. As people become more generalized, it makes balancing work across different disciplines easier. People on the business side develop close personal relationships with people on the implementation side; you remove the us versus them dichotomy and get a smoothly functioning, efficient process.

Seeing the group as a community, it becomes easy to create a small workgroup within the community on an as-needed basis to complete some particular task. These small workgroups can come and go without the problems of team forming, because everyone knows each other within the community. Finally, because you have a whole community with deep knowledge of the domain, if a particular project gets behind, you can add people to the project without having to spend a lot of time getting them up-to-speed.

You start by identifying your capital assets, service offerings, and groups of related capital assets that you want to manage as one (for example a back office capital asset group that handles all back office capital assets, not just Microsoft Office). Once you know what your capital assets and services are, you create a community around each asset, service, or asset group. This could be 30-100 people depending on the size of the asset and number of users. This community typically will include people in roles of sales, marketing, solution anthropology, implementation, test, deployment, and support.

The community is seated together in a large space and dedicated to that capital asset, capital asset group, or service offering. Within the community, there may be two kinds of managers - an asset steward managing the business and user needs (which I will call the asset management team) and a technical manager managing implementation and support (which I will call the technical team). Sometimes the product management team is seated separately from the technical team, but is still physically nearby so as to promote ease of communication.

The asset steward typically has a team of people who help create the vision of the future by doing activities such as market research, focus groups, competitor analysis, trade shows, and solution anthropology to determine what their users want. They are also responsible for communication to the users about the asset, including change management and training. The amount of time spent on these activities varies depending on whether the asset is used internally, sold as a product in a slow moving market, or sold as a product in a fast moving market.

The asset steward maintains the vision of the future expressed as a prioritized queue of work to be done for this asset. The asset steward is responsible for the ROI of the asset.

Solution Anthropologists are very important members of the asset management team. They are the voice of the user and work directly with end users to determine their needs using tools such as observation, interviews, analysis, UI mockups, and cognitive walkthroughs. They are the liaison to the technical team, spending about half time with each team, asset management and technical.

The technical manager has a team of people who create, enhance, maintain and support the asset. The technical manager is responsible for organizing the work of the technical team and for the technical vision of the asset.

The technical manager is typically supported by a team of architects who do technical research, product analysis, trade shows, and other activities to stay up to date with technology trends and new possibilities. They collaborate closely with the asset steward to ensure the asset vision and technical vision are aligned. The work of the architects is similar when the asset is a product for sale or something used internally.

The technical team does all the work of creating, installing, configuring, enhancing, and maintaining the product; in particular, there are no separate operations, devOps, or maintenance teams, they are all part of the technical team.

Technical and customer support are very important members of the technical team. They talk with users all the time and are very much in tune with how the users are using the asset in real life. The support members of the technical team keep the technical manager apprised of defect reports and feature requests that users submit.

Though I talked about two teams it was for convenience to show the different roles and activities within the community. Since all of these people are part of the same community, they can and do move around to different roles within the community based on their interest, skills, and career goals. A Java programmer might spend some time in support or a UX designer doing solution anthropology might want to learn iOS programming. Not only can they, but wise managers will assign people to new roles for some time in order to build community knowledge. Using the practice of paired work makes this not only feasible but relatively easy and low cost.

With paired work, every task is done by two people working side by side as if they were one person. One person is taking a support call while the other monitors the call, then they switch. One person programs while the other watches, then they switch. When using this approach for training, the person learning the skill does the work while the more experienced person monitors.

Because the task is typically completed faster and with much higher quality, paired work does not cost more than having individuals working alone. Over time, pairing people to work on every task reduces the lifetime cost of maintaining the asset. (Note that pairing is used with knowledge work, which is the kind of work where you do a lot of thinking.)

Since the same community does work that is capitalized and work that is expensed, it is important to keep track of where to account for work. This can be relatively easily handled by creating work packages tagged as either capital or expense so that community members know where to charge their time for that work package. In some cases, a person's whole job is either capitalized or expensed so that makes it even easier. You always know the capital asset to associate the work with because everyone in the community is working on the same capital asset.

In some cases, where the company's capital assets are dependent on a common infrastructure, there may need to be a community that maintains the infrastructure as their asset. If there is no user interface for this infrastructure, then architects from the different communities that use the asset may be the voice of the user for this infrastructure community.

When the capital asset is used internally, many people are tempted to include the users as members of the community. This is usually not feasible since the user's job is not to maintain the asset, it is to use the asset. The user's input is extremely important and it is captured the same way we capture the user needs for products we sell, through the Solution Anthropology and Support roles in the capital asset community.

Create Guilds for Specialties

There is still a need for specialist knowledge, but putting all the specialists together in a group creates blockages in workflow when other people have to wait for their knowledge. It can also lead to a situation where the specialists are out of touch with the real business of the company. They have a lot of theoretical knowledge but do not know how to put it into practice anymore.

The specialists will be spread out into the capital asset communities providing their specialized knowledge in place as part of the daily work of the company. Some knowledge, such as the enterprise architecture or data models, is shared across the company and needs to be maintained. This can be done through the creation of guilds.

While everyone works daily for the community, the guild meets part time on a regular basis, such as one hour once a week. Anyone with interest can be part of the guild, thus promoting knowledge sharing and professional growth opportunities. For example, you might have an architecture guild whose members meet for purposes such as review the current enterprise architecture to see if it still makes sense, someone shares some research she recently did on big data, there is a short hack-a-thon on design patterns, or someone shares an architectural insight he had while working on a capital asset. The guild may hold longer events, such as a two day workshop to revise company architectural standards, or a five day class on being an architect.

Guilds do take up some time that is not being spent directly on supporting a capital asset, but this time is needed to support cross-company information, standards, and guidelines that everyone will use. Creating guilds whose members come from all the different communities is a way to do that work without removing the specialists from the day-to-day work of the company. It also provides a way for others to grow in that specialized knowledge, thus preventing the one deep problem found in so many companies. Guilds are a primary mechanism for supporting continuous improvement.

Organize careers around goals not static job descriptions

Technical and asset managers throughout the company collaborate to support the development paths of the people who work for them. This collaboration enables individuals to move to different communities within the company based on their interests and career goals.

The current practice of creating job classifications and progressions has led to specialization and rigidity of corporate structures. So many companies (even in the Fortune 50) tell me that some critical knowledge in their company is "one deep". This means only one person knows that information. This is a high risk situation for the company. For the company to be agile, the workforce should be agile as well.

When you have an agile workforce, you can easily balance work loads around the company. You do not have to worry about knowledge being one deep because any set of information is known by many people. You do not get there by creating specialized job descriptions. Instead, your career paths are designed to reward people for gaining broad knowledge. The career progression I outline below also solves the problem of what to do with senior technical people who do not want to be managers but have nowhere else to go to "progress" in their career.

As a start, you hire people for a good fit with your company culture. Specific skills can be learned as needed, and your company and the people you hire should expect that your employees will continue learning throughout their career. In the modern world, and especially if you embrace Agile practices, one of the most important things you need to watch for in an interview is the ability to work collaboratively with others. Menlo Innovations published a paper on Extreme Interviews, which is the technique they use to discover people who play nicely with others. A Google search will turn it up, or you can go to the website for this book to get a copy.

Next you get rid of all the levels of jobs. Job descriptions should be fairly general. You are not going to base raises or promotions on these job descriptions, but instead use them to outline the kind of work performed by a particular role. A manager has to know what the company vision is and what skill sets will best help the company reach its goals. A manager reviews the current skills of an employee and with the employee determines how that person can enhance his/her knowledge and experience in valuable skills or acquire new skills. The manager and employee set goals. How well the employee progresses toward those goals is the basis for the performance review and any raises.

In addition to the goal setting and goal review, the manager asks members of the person's community to review his or her work. In general, a manager should look for people that this person has worked closely with. Here you are basically trying to determine if the person is still a good fit and is working out well.

An easy approach is just to say to a group of people, what if we could only keep half of you? Who do you want to keep? Their answers will tell you who they perceive as the most valuable members of the community. Similarly, members of the community are asked to review the manager's work. Some people call these 360 degree reviews.

In this model, you do not rank employees against each other. Each person is only compared to him or her self. Those who do not make good progress toward their goals, and especially those that the community finds less valuable, are providing low value to the company, which can be addressed in many ways.

This model makes many people uncomfortable because there is no clear ranking of people, no hierarchy. A person may lead a particular work effort because she has the vision, even though she may have much less experience than other members of the team. The next time someone else has the vision and takes a leadership role on that work effort. People lead because they are good at it, not because they got "promoted" into a leadership position.

I know this kind of approach for promotions and career growth is legal and possible in the USA because I know actual companies who have followed this approach for 20 years and more. The USA has at will employment, which is not necessarily the case elsewhere. In the rest of the world, it is possible that labor laws may make this approach difficult to impossible to implement.

The most extreme version of this approach I know of, the people who work together hire new employees to work in their community, fire people who are not working out, and review each other for raises. Management is not involved. You might think everyone will give everyone else a raise every year, but it does not work out that way over time. The nature of a community is to protect the community, not necessarily individuals within the community. Slackers are quickly discovered and let go. People who do not want to learn and grow find they do not get raises and also generally leave.

Incorporating remote workers

Agile works best when people are physically together. Humans are genetically evolved for face-to-face interactions. It is what we have done for most of human history. When people are not together to work, there are many inefficiencies due to lack of communication, poor communication, and handoffs. Having said that, global distribution of work is a reality that we cannot ignore.

When the community is distributed, we try to have any particular workgroup (2-5 people implementing one work package) be physically co-located. When work packages are well defined, this greatly reduces the need for collaboration across geographies, which is a major source of inefficiency.

It is still important for members of the community to spend time together, so several times a year the remote people should come to the location of the main community and spend time working with them in person on site. This is important in order to make collaboration as smooth as possible, to promote mutual understanding of the capital asset they support, and to retain employees by developing personal relationships between members of the community.

When the users are in a different place than the implementers, the Solution Anthropology team can bridge the gap by spending time with the users at their location and spending time with the implementers at their location. You will need to find people to do this role who don't mind and are able to do a lot of travel. I have been in this role in the past and have a lot of stamps on my passport to show for it!

When time zones are close together (no more than 3 hours difference), working in a telepresence location is a very effective way to make the work be more efficient. Telepresence is so good today, it is like you are in a room together. There is a real cost to this, and some inefficiencies due to the hours not spent together, but this is much better than collaborating by handing off documents.

When you have a situation where one person is in Denver, two people are in India, another one person is in Ireland, and they have to do some work together, the most efficient way to handle this is to define the smallest amount of work they have to do together and get them all together in one location to do the work. The work will be completed in maybe ¼ the time it would take when they are all working in different locations. It really is that much more efficient to be in the same physical location and in the same time zone when working together. The rest of the time they will work independently and not try to form a team.

Many distributed communities find it works very well to get the whole community together for a week at least once a year. This week can be used for activities such as workshops or training, managers can share the vision of the future for the company and for the capital asset they manage, and it is a good time for social events outside of work. The community will work together much more efficiently after spending time together as a community. It actually works so well, that if your community is all in the same location, an event once a year for the whole community still enhances the work of the community. It may be just 1-2 days instead of a week, but the community is doing something all together.

Chapter 22

Structure the Work for Agile

N ow that the workforce is structured to support Agile, you want to consider how the work itself is organized. As much as possible you want to think about continuous streams of work instead of the start and stop of projects. At the same time, some work does fit the project model better, especially when working with vendors. You also want to consider the different ways you measure success. In this chapter, we cover these topics:

1. Organize the work as releases
2. What Project Managers do in Agile
3. Working with vendors
4. Get real user feedback and involvement
5. Agile metrics

Organize the Work as Releases

When communities of people are organized around capital assets which have a long lifetime, it does not make sense to organize their work as projects which have a short term focus. Instead work is organized around releases. This seems a minor distinction, but it does have profound consequences because how we think about the asset and how we think about success are different.

The community is working continuously on the capital asset. At points in time, we want to make that asset available to users and capitalize it. A release point is that point in time.

Since there are no projects for this work, there is no cost associated with managing a portfolio of projects, starting up a project, and ending a project. Instead we manage a portfolio of assets and fund the community for each asset with a yearly budget based on expected ROI for that asset. Of course you also have to fund functions that are purely expense and not part of a capital asset community, such as keeping the building clean, running payroll, guiding the corporate direction, and so on.

At well-defined points in time, the asset steward and the technical manager for the capital asset or service offering they manage meet to plan release points. The asset steward brings the queue of desired features and the technical manager brings the queue of defect reports, user requested features, and updates recommended by the architects.

Typically the asset steward decides the rhythm of releases. He or she will consider factors such as keeping up-to-date with changes in the market balanced against a need to not overwhelm the users with too many changes in too short a time. Or there may be a desire to release new features ahead of a competitor or just before a conference or trade show. The technical manager may have some good technical reasons for modifying the release schedule, such as waiting to release a particular feature until a technology that better supports it becomes available, but technical reasons should usually be subordinate to business reasons.

The managers share their goals for what they want to accomplish by the release date, select a target date, and make an initial selection of features, defect fixes, and updates to be implemented in this cycle. Then the managers talk with their teams about whether or not the targets are feasible. If the asset management team or the technical team thinks there is too much work, they help the managers determine what they can do.

Work is not scheduled to fill every available hour of time. Not more than 80% of the team's time is "budgeted" for work. The rest is needed for meetings, sick days, holidays, vacations, and to provide a buffer against unexpected problems or emergency injects of critical work. Also, the team is only expected to work at most 40 hours in a week (some companies are even experimenting quite successfully with a 32 hour work week for knowledge workers). This lets everyone work constantly over long periods without burnout. Some managers schedule only 50% of the team's time to do the work for the release. They may know from experience that their team always underestimates the work or experience suggests they will get many injects during the release cycle.

The managers meet again to finalize the queue of work to be released in the next cycle. They may adjust priorities, add or remove items from the queue, or change the release date. At this point, the whole community knows what needs to be done and by when. They start to work.

During the time period when the features to be released are being implemented, the technical manager may choose to have some implementers work on critical defects. The fixes to these defects may be released independently of planned new features to solve immediate problems, or the asset steward may wish to add (inject) a feature a competitor just released or that she discovered was extremely important to the users. These are reasons why all of the team's time is not budgeted up front; it allows for flexibility to handle the unforeseen.

What Project Managers do in Agile

In the corporate structure outlined in this section, there is still a need for projects and project managers. While managing a long lived capital asset is best done by a community (and not a series of projects), there is work that needs to be done that is well defined, relatively short lived, and infrequently done. Projects are a perfect fit for this kind of work.

Projects are often formed around events or third party products. This could be things such as installing or upgrading Microsoft Office, putting together the company presence at a trade show, organizing the yearly user conference, or removing a decommissioned mainframe. While these kinds of things should be part of a long term vision, and are still implemented by members of the community, the actual work is short and self-contained. The short term goals of a project team are ideal for managing this kind of work.

A project structure is a good fit for work that can be planned well in advance, with a fixed budget, scope, and end date that are very unlikely to change. Project managers are trained to deliver to the budget, schedule, and scope. It is not their job to keep the long term vision nor to know the market, but that is not required for this kind of work. The project managers for the projects come from within the capital asset community and work closely with the asset steward and the technical manager of the community.

You do not need to make a fast response to the market when installing the latest version of Lotus Notes company wide. Nor is this ongoing work – it is IBM's problem to maintain Lotus Notes, not yours. This is a good fit for a project. Having said that, there is still someone responsible for the long term back office vision – the asset steward for the back office capital asset community. A project to update Lotus Notes (or replace it) would be commissioned by the asset steward as part of the work that needs to be done to maintain the set of capital assets for back office work.

Given a particular budget, the asset steward will allocate some of that money to specific projects and the rest to ongoing work on the capital asset. This balances the need for necessary work such as upgrades against the need to be flexible to market demands. It also enables the asset manager to balance between short term ROI and the need to keep the lifetime cost of the asset low.

For a group such as a back office community, it may be that most of their work is done as a series of projects, because the needs of the users are slow to change, relatively easy to predict in advance, and unlikely to change. A community supporting capital assets used by sales people will most likely work off a yearly budget with regular releases and not do projects because their users are often asking for new things, they cannot predict in advance what they will want, and they change their minds frequently. Sales people are being driven by the market.

Working with Vendors

When working with vendors, a careful design of the contract can ensure your company still has the ability to be agile, no matter how the other company works. Relatively short delivery cycles with frequent demonstrations of working solutions, proof of conformance to quality standards, and delivery of test scripts with the code (automated if possible) should all be part of the contract.

This is a kind of design by contract. As long as you carefully define the contract, and the vendor fulfills it, their work should just "slot into" the work done inside your company. To make this work the best, you want to eliminate dependencies between the work performed in house and the work performed by the vendor.

At the same time, you want a representative from the vendor team to work closely with the in-house staff, ideally on-site with them. This vendor representative can keep you up-to-date on progress, demonstrate the work his team has completed, and take feedback from your company back to his team.

In order to be agile, contracted work should be of short duration. While the overall contract may be many months, you should define short work packages for delivery. Work closely with the vendor to determine the feasible length of time, but the goal should always be that they work for one month or less and at the end of that time they deliver some working solution. It may not be a complete solution from the point of view of the overall effort, but the work that is complete should function as required and be production quality.

You are trying to avoid a situation where the vendor takes your requirements, disappears for a few months, and then you are stuck with whatever they deliver. In that situation, you are unable to address issues earlier, nor can you easily make change.

With the popularity of agile, you are very likely to be able to find vendors who will work with you this way. Be sure the contract you write with procurement does not require you to lock in the requirements up front. Rather you define the requirements a bit at a time.

It is good to describe the contract more as a bucket of money that represents the maximum you will spend with this vendor. The vendor works with you to estimate each work package, and you pay on delivery of the work packages you and the vendor agreed on.

Sometimes you will have to be more explicit. For example, if you are doing a big SAP installation, you will identify up front which SAP modules you will be licensing and installing. A lot of the data modeling will also have to be done up front because of dependencies between the modules based on that data. At the same time, there are vendors who will install, configure, and test SAP modules incrementally, so you do not have to wait for a year or more to find out if anything works.

Real User Feedback and Involvement

A very important feature of agile is to get feedback from actual users of your products. This is completely different from getting feedback from project sponsors about what they want.

When the asset or service is being provided to users inside your company, there is no reason to avoid getting the users involved in developing and refining the asset or service offering. Too often, the implementers get information from someone such as a business sponsor and do not talk with the actual users. Or they "kidnap" one user, typically a subject matter expert, and have that person represent the whole group of users. Often the subject matter expert has not done the day-to-day work for many years. In neither case is the team getting feedback from the actual people using the asset or service day-to-day.

It is important to apply Solution Anthropology inside your company to find out what the actual users need. The Solution Anthropology team members spend time with the actual users at the users' location to determine the real needs and to find out the real issues. A variety of observational and interview techniques are used to elicit requirements and to determine that the proposed solution is a good one. The goal of the Solution Anthropology team is that the solution delights the users. This is good inside your company because this means the users will be the most efficient and effective with the provided solutions.

When working with users outside your company, the work is more challenging. As much as possible, you still want to use a Solution Anthropology team to go to the locations where people are using your products and services to find the issues in the users' native environment. I have seen many problems over the years with products and services because the company made assumptions about what the users wanted, or how the users would use the product, and the assumptions were wrong. Better to get information directly from real users and use that information to create solutions for them.

This is especially important in areas such as mobile or wearables, where users have many choices and will quickly abandon your products if they are not as friendly or usable as a competitors. One of the identified reasons for the slow adoption of wearables, and the reason 1/3 of users abandon them within a few months, is that the devices are not pleasing to the users; they are not attractive and they are difficult to use. If your company is in those markets and uses Solution Anthropology to find out what delights the users, then you could easily dominate that space.

In addition to Solution Anthropology, your customers are more and more expecting to be involved with your company. You need to be in social media, monitoring what is said and responding. But avoid the common "canned answer" that many companies are using. After reading a social media page full of responses that are all essentially the same, no one cares anymore. This does you more harm than good. Senior people who are empowered to make decisions should be the ones responding in the social space. It is that important.

Look for ways to invite suggestions from your users. What would they like to see from your company? Do not limit this to tradeshows, but provide a digital way for users to contact you. If you are going to do surveys, get someone who knows what they are doing to create the survey for you. I have seen far too many truly awful surveys from prominent companies. They are clearly designed to give the company an answer they are expecting instead of allowing the user to tell the company what the user wants the company to know.

Consider using a variation of a crowd-funding platform where you list products, services or features you are considering developing. Give your users accounts with "play money" and let them buy a feature. When you reach your minimum goal, you know you have a big enough market to develop that feature. You could even let users put in real money, and your funding goal gives you the money you need to develop the product, service, or feature.

What works really well is to find a way to gamify interactions. Adding features such as points and rankings to the systems you use to collect user feedback encourages your users to provide the feedback you seek.

Agile Metrics

For the most part, in an agile company we stop measuring project schedule and budget. What is of far more interest is measuring directly the goals we are trying to achieve. Often this is Return on Investment (ROI), but there may be other goals as well, such as maximizing throughput of a value stream or minimizing the length of a value stream.

Every large company I have worked for asks for an estimated ROI for a project before a budget is approved. Most of the ROI numbers I have seen are complete fictions. I have yet to find a large company that measures the actual ROI once the project is completed to see if it was achieved. And yet this is much more important than meeting an estimated schedule or budget.

Small companies tend to measure actual ROI. They do not have the leeway in their budget to be wrong a lot, and so they quickly determine what is providing the necessary ROI, and get rid of what is not. Their budgets are more limited, so each investment needs to provide value.

Sometimes we are not as worried about the ROI of a specific effort. You may have an effort to attract more business, and while that particular effort does not provide a profit, you plan to sell more to these new customers over time and so the gain is later. In this case you measure and limit the cost to acquire a new customer rather than measuring the ROI of the effort.

Many companies measure throughput of their value streams. This can be useful in a service organization, as long as you also measure other things such as quality of the interaction or customer satisfaction. A customer service representative can show great throughput if they just say "no" all the time and hang up, but your customers will not be happy. A different measurement may be more effective, and that is to measure the time it takes to satisfy a request balanced with high customer satisfaction. You may have goals for the average time to satisfy a customer is 5 minutes or less, for example. The customer is the person who gets to say if they were satisfied or not.

The really important thing about metrics is not to measure one thing. Look for a set of metrics that balance each other to get the results you desire. Then let the metrics tell you the real story.

Too often projects are only measured on schedule and budget, and not quality, because if quality were included it would prove that the schedule and budget were underestimated, sometimes greatly. No one wants to hear that, so quality is not measured. Instead, every project finishes on time and on budget and we schedule a follow on project to fix the quality issues. Instead of that, you could also measure quality and let the metrics tell you the real story. Then you have the real data to know what the schedule and budget should be to do it right the first time.

Chapter 23

Agile Infrastructure

The final set of things to consider are in the larger infrastructure of your company. Various tools make being Agile much easier. You also have to consider the value stream that the implementation teams are part of. What might be happening in another part of the value stream that is making the implementation of features less efficient? Topics in this chapter are:

1. Tools to support agile
2. Optimize the whole value stream
3. First steps to becoming a more Agile company

Tools to Support Agile

For corporate agility, you need tool support. Automated testing is a necessity in today's fast moving markets. A staging area for product that is complete but for whatever reason you do not want to release it to market just yet provides a lot of flexibility. This is especially true when the product is to be used internally. This staging area can be potentially be used by a small set of users doing their "real job" (that is, this is not a testing scenario but they are actually working) in order to find the more subtle errors before it goes live. This is sometimes referred to as ad hoc testing.

If you do have actual users working in the staging area, locating the users in an area with a mirrored wall can provide the opportunity to observe the users without them being disturbed. This also gives you the opportunity to invite executives to observe, most of whom have no idea what the users actually do or want. This can be very educational. More than one executive has completely changed attitude when he discovered that he was really out of touch with the users and their needs.

If you do not have everyone physically collocated, telepresence is rapidly becoming necessary. People are too used to it in their personal lives (Skype, Hangouts, etc.) to give it up at work and the efficiency gains are substantial. Watch out for cost though. A poorly written contract with a vendor could lead to quite high and unexpected costs.

One team I know had telepresence on all day so their widespread members could work together. But the company's contract with the service provider was a charge per person per hour. The first month's bill was very high and the team had to find another way to work together.

Telepresence should be set up in a separate room not in a large open area where everyone is working. It is too distracting to everyone else. A team relying on telepresense should have their own room to work in.

Walls covered with Idea Paint make it very easy for people to hold impromptu discussions or design sessions. Just be sure people can get to the walls, that they are not blocked with furniture or covered with posters or paintings. Make ad hoc meetings even easier with high speed, high bandwidth wireless throughout the site, notebook computers or tablets, movable furniture, and ad hoc meeting spaces. Use cloth tape on the floor to mark out fire lanes and other places where furniture cannot be placed.

Forget the idea of all digital – make things physical, touchable, movable, get people out of their heads and talking, get people out of their seats and walking. No email, IM, or telephones for most people. If we are in a room together, we don't need any of that and it is just distracting. If people really must have email, then train them to check it once a day, either first thing in the morning or at the end of the day. Turn it off otherwise.

In terms of physical space, I have seen two configurations work pretty well. Assuming you have a community all in one large area together, make the space large enough that individual teams have a wide area of physical separation so that they are not constantly overhearing each other's conversation. Rolling white boards help visually divide up the space and give each team or workgroup a place to show their work.

Alternatively, put the community in an area with a lot of rooms and one large common area with furniture for ad hoc meetings. Each individual workgroup of perhaps 10 or so people has their own room to work in with plenty of whiteboards and telepresence if needed. The common area is nice for things such as a weekly community wide standup meeting.

Optimize the Whole Value Stream

A value stream is how your company services those who use your company (customers, vendors, employees, community organizations, etc.). A value stream starts with someone who makes a request to your company and ends with the fulfillment of that request. Everything from start to finish is part of the value stream. The flow through the value stream is what you want to optimize for greatest overall corporate efficiency. This is much more than making the implementation team more efficient; the whole value stream must be examined.

Requests and the ultimate responses define many sizes of value streams. A request/response value stream could be someone asking for a balance in their account and getting it, a customer purchasing a product and receiving it, someone reporting a defect in a product and getting a work around, someone reporting a defect in a product and getting a new version of the product with the defect fixed, someone requesting a new feature and getting a new version of the product with that new feature, or even someone requesting a new product and the new product is delivered to them.

In general your value stream will include a way to request work (project proposal, feature list under consideration, input from market research), a way to approve funding for work, scheduling the work, doing the work, and releasing the finished work. In a large company, there can be many people and many processes involved in this value stream. If all you do is make the implementation team more efficient, you may find they are spending a lot of time waiting for work to come to them. And so the front end processes need to be made more efficient as well.

In a customer driven world, we want to reduce the time from request to response to be as short as we can while still delivering quality. This is good for customers, vendors, and employees leading to a stronger company overall.

Value streams are typically described as starting with a request from outside the company, but when managing capital assets that are used internally, we can apply the same concept. The value streams start with a request from outside the capital asset community and end when that request is satisfied. If you have a community managing the back office group of capital assets, then the value stream starts with a request from another employee and ends when the request is satisfied.

It is important to note that the satisfaction of a request might be the answer "No".

First Steps to Becoming a More Agile Company

When considering an Agile implementation, there is no "one size fits all" solution. You need to assess where your company is today, and consider your needs or the problems you are trying to solve. Then you can select practices to try. You always want to measure the results to see if you received the benefit you desired.

The Big Three Management practices in section 1 are always good to do. While they do take time for everyone to learn, they typically do not require big structural or procedural changes in your company. I have used just those three relatively simple practices to turn around a huge waterfall project where everyone (users, sponsors, implementers) mistrusted everyone else and the project was failing. I could not change most things about the project, but I could get the work defined as relatively small, nearly independent work packages on a prioritized queue, regular demonstration of progress, and incremental delivery. The results were magical.

If you cannot do anything else at this time, just do those three practices and measure the results. I think you will see the magic as well.

About the Author

Geri Schneider Winters is a polymath with a wide range of interests. She loves bringing all that knowledge to bear when solving large, complex problems. Because of that, she is frequently found guiding business transformations at large companies.

In support of her business transformation work, Ms. Winters has studied and put into practice domains such as analysis, science of the brain, hypnosis, psychology, influence and advocacy, anthropology, philosophy, adult education, communication, marketing, interviewing, and a wide range of documentation techniques.

Ms. Winters explores her creative side with hobbies in healthy living, home brewing, cooking, photography, writing, book publishing, website creation, video production, singing, acting, and musical theater production. She has a deep love of the natural sciences and has been known to read physics "for fun", but admits to being "horrible" at tennis, basketball, and statistics.

Ms. Winters lives in a redwood forest on the Northern California coast with her husband and cats. She shares her property with deer, bunnies, skunks, foxes, many kinds of birds, and at least one bobcat. She is also within the territory of a mountain lion, but has not seen it (and does not want to).

Other Books by this Author

The original edition of Applying Use Cases was the first published book devoted to the topic of use cases - and an instant best seller. Schneider and Winters showed us not only how to write use cases, but what to do with them throughout a full incremental development lifecycle. The second edition was updated to UML 2.0 and expanded to show how to write use cases for business, and how to flow business use cases into software.

Applying Use Cases: A Practical Guide has been used in professional training in business analysis, Agile development, software architecture, and project management. It has also been the required text for project management courses at many universities.

This popular book has been continuously in print worldwide for over 15 years. It is available from Addision-Wesley Professional in US English, Polish, and Japanese editions.